## INTRODUCTION TO THE FIRST EDITION

We have gathered together this collection of recipes from the Orkney Islands to let you savour the very best in Orkney cookery.

To produce the book, we circulated all the Orkney branches of the Scottish Women's Rural Institute, hotels and restaurants and everyone we felt could make an interesting contribution.

We also encouraged people to devise original recipes, using local produce such as meat, seafood, cheese, grain, sweetmeats, whisky etc. and give it an Orkney name. The response was excellent.

In making the fnal selection, we tried to give priority to what we considered to be original recipes with a distinctive Orkney flavour and we hope you will test and taste what we consider to be an exciting new collection to take into your kitchen.

Special thanks are due to:

Mr Gerry Meyer of *The Orcadian* who kindly printed details of our quest and brought in many contributions.

Mr Howie Firth of BBC Radio Orkney, who broadcast an appeal for recipes with great results.

Mr Tam MacPhail of Stromness Books and Prints and Mr John Leonard of Kirkwall, who kindly distributed leaflets to their bookshop customers.

All this effort contributed to the final production and we are indeed indebted to everyone concerned.

D1424823

# Recipes from the Orkney Islands

### Edited by Eileen Wolfe

## Steve Savage

LONDON AND EDINBURGH

Steve Savage Publishers Ltd
The Old Truman Brewery
91 Brick Lane
LONDON
E1 6QL

www.savagepublishers.com

Published in Great Britain by Steve Savage Publishers Ltd 2005
Reprinted 2008

First published by Gordon Wright Publishing Ltd 1978
Copyright © Steve Savage Publishers Ltd 1978, 2005

ISBN: 978-1-904246-15-2

Typeset by Steve Savage Publishers Ltd
Printed and bound by The Cromwell Press Ltd

# Contents

Soup 7

Fish 19

Meat 27

Poultry and game 37

Savoury 45

Vegetables and salads 55

Sauces 63

Dessert 71

Baking 83

Preserves 104

Confectionery 114

Home-brew 118

Household hints 124

Index 126

## *NOTE ON MEASURES*

The original recipes used traditional measures, and these are included in this edition, alongside the approximate metric equivalents.

# SOUP

## *Orcadian Oatmeal Soup*

1 large onion
2 small carrots
1 leek
A little turnip
  or cabbage
25g (1 oz)
  oatmeal
600ml (1 pint)
  stock
450ml (³/₄ pint)
  milk
Seasoning
Fat

### Method

1. Prepare and dice all the vegetables.

2. Toss the vegetables in the melted fat until coated.

3. Add the oatmeal and fry for a few minutes.

4. Add the stock and the seasoning and simmer for 45 minutes.

5. The soup can now be sieved or liquidised if required.

6. Add the milk and reheat before serving.

**H. Firth, Kirkwall**

## *Scotch Broth*

450–675g (1–1¹/₂
  lb) mutton,
  chopped
2 medium carrots
2 medium onions
¹/₂ medium
  turnip
45ml (3 table-
  spoons) pearl
  barley
300ml (1 cup)
  dried peas
3.6 litres (6
  pints) of water
Salt and pepper

### Method

1. Soak the barley and peas overnight in cold water.

2. Put the peas, barley, meat and water into a pan with a pinch of salt.

3. Cover pan and bring slowly to the boil.

4. Skim carefully.

5. Peel and dice the vegetables and add to the pan.

6. Simmer for 1¹/₂–2 hours, then season to taste.

**J. Wilkie, Evie**

## Holm Vegetable Soup

1 small carrot
1 small turnip
1 small onion
1/2 a leek
1 stick celery
1.2 litres (2 pints) water
300ml (1/2 pint) milk
25g (1 oz) flour
1/2 small bay leaf
Salt and pepper

### Method

1. Shred the vegetables.

2. Melt the butter and toss the vegetables in it.

3. Add the bay leaf and water and boil until the vegetables are tender.

4. Mix the flour and milk together and add to the pan. Boil for a few minutes to cook the flour, stirring continuously.

5. Take out bay leaf, season well and serve hot.

**D. Laughton, Holm**


## Red Potage

225g (1/2 lb) haricot beans
25g (1 oz) butter
1 large onion
1 beetroot
4 small tomatoes
1 stick celery
1.8 litres (3 pints) water, or stock

### Method

1. Peel onion, beetroot and tomatoes. Roughly chop all the vegetables.

2. Melt butter and add all ingredients. Cook gently for a few minutes.

3. Add water or stock.

4. Season and simmer for two hours.

5. Sieve, reheat and serve piping hot.

**Mrs Findlay, Stromness**

# Cabbage Soup

1 large cabbage
50g (2 oz) butter
1.2 litres
(2 pints) milk
2 large potatoes,
thinly sliced
Seasoning

## Method

1. Wash the cabbage well and let it stand in salted water for one hour.

2. Rinse the cabbage and shred it finely.

3. Melt the butter in a stewpan, put in the cabbage and stir until the cabbage has absorbed all the butter.

4. Add enough water to cover and stew till tender.

5. Add the potatoes, and when they are cooked, mash them up to thicken the soup.

6. Season, add the milk and boil up to serve.

*P. Johnston, Stromness*

# Spring Soup

1.2 litres (2
pints) stock
2.5ml ($\frac{1}{2}$ tea-
spoon) castor
sugar
15ml (1 table-
spoon) rice
15ml (1 tablespoon)
each: shredded
lettuce, carrot and
turnip (diced)
Seasoning

## Method

1. Boil the stock, add the rice, carrots and turnip and cook for 15 minutes.

2. Add the lettuce, sugar and seasoning and simmer till tender.

*L. Grieve, Kirkwall*

# Tomato Soup

900g (2 lb)
  tomatoes
1 large onion
15g (½ oz) butter
1.2 litres (2
  pints) stock
50g (2 oz) lean
  cooked ham,
  chopped
15ml (1 table-
  spoon) sago
2.5ml (½ tea-
  spoon) sugar
Seasoning

## Method

1. Slice the tomatoes and onions and fry them with the ham in the butter for 20 minutes, then rub through a fine sieve.

2. To this purée, add the stock, sago, sugar and salt and pepper to taste.

3. Bring to the boil and simmer until the sago is clear.

**I. Hourston, Kirkwall**

# Cauliflower Soup

2.4 litres
  (4 pints) clear
  stock
Small cauliflower
Parmesan cheese
Cayenne pepper
Chopped parsley

## Method

1. Pour boiling water over the cauliflower then plunge it into cold water.

2. Cut the cauliflower into small pieces, and boil in salted water until tender. Strain and put the cauliflower into the soup tureen.

3. Bring the stock to the boil and pour it over the cauliflower.

4. Sprinkle with cayenne pepper and finely chopped parsley and serve with grated Parmesan cheese.

**E. Harvey, Stromness**

# Chicken Broth

1 boiling chicken
50g (2 oz) rice
1 carrot
1 leek
1 onion
2.4 litres (4
   pints) water
Seasoning
1 blade of mace
Parsley

## Method

1. Simmer the chicken in the water for 1½ hours.

2. Remove the chicken from the water and add salt.

3. Chop the vegetables and add them to the stock with the rice and the blade of mace. Boil for a further 30 minutes. Skim when necessary.

4. Season to taste and serve with a sprinkling of chopped parsley.

*T. Moar, Birsay*


# Carrot Soup

5 carrots
2 onions
2 sticks celery
Turnip
5ml (1 teaspoon)
   sugar
Knob of butter
Stock
Seasoning

## Method

1. In 1.8 litres (3 pints) of well-seasoned stock boil the chopped vegetables.

2. Pulp the boiled vegetables through a sieve, add the butter and sugar.

3. Boil for 15 minutes to serve piping hot.

*K. Wilson, Stromness*

# Potato Soup

450g (1 lb) potatoes
1 large onion
25g (1 oz) butter
25g (1 oz) flour
1.8 litres (3 pints) weak stock
30ml (2 tablespoons) cream
10ml (1 dessertspoon) finely chopped parsley
Pepper and salt

## Method

1. Slice the onion finely and put it into a saucepan with the butter. Fry without browning for 15 minutes, stirring constantly.

2. Add the stock, and the potatoes cut into slices. Stir until soup boils, skim, and continue boiling until the potatoes are tender.

3. Rub all through a sieve, season, and put back into the saucepan to reboil.

4. Mix the flour with the cream and stir into the soup.

5. Add the finely chopped parsley and serve.

*E. Harvey, Stromness*


# Winter Vegetable Soup

Turnip
Carrot
Potato
Onion
Celery
Sweet herbs
Butter
Seasoning

## Method

1. Melt a large knob of butter in a pan and toss equal quantities of chopped vegetables until they are brown.

2. Add water, seasoning and herbs and boil until tender.

3. Serve with toasted bread.

*L. Young, Stromness*

# Scots Kale

300ml (1 cup)
  barley
225g (½ lb)
  fresh beef
2 leeks
Kale
Salt
Water

## Method

1. Put the barley in cold water and bring to the boil. Remove any scum.

2. Chop the beef finely and add to the soup pot with a little salt. Boil for 3 hours.

3. Chop the kale and leeks and add to the soup. Continue boiling until the greens are tender.

4. Season to taste.

**N. Wylie, Kirkwall**

# Scottish Herring Soup

2 small onions,
  finely chopped
4 herrings,
  cleaned and
  boned
25g (1 oz) butter
50g (2 oz) mush-
  rooms
400g (14 oz) can
  tomatoes
600ml (1 pint)
  water
45ml (3 table-
  spoons) malt
  vinegar
Salt and pepper

## Method

1. Cut the herrings into 1cm (½-inch) pieces and add with other ingredients to water.

2. Bring to the boil and simmer gently for about 30 minutes until onions are ready.

**H. Garson, Sandwick**

# Beetroot Soup

2 beetroots
3 onions
1.2 litres (2 pints) stock
45ml (3 tablespoons) vinegar
15ml (1 tablespoon) brown sugar
Seasoning

## Method

1. Boil the beetroots until tender and rub off the skins.

2. Chop the beetroot and onions finely and add to the stock.

3. Stir in the vinegar and sugar and bring to the boil.

4. Season to taste.

**K. Wilson, Stromness**

# Brussels Sprouts Soup

450g (1 lb) Brussels sprouts
75g (3 oz) butter
25g (1 oz) flour
1.2 litres (2 pints) white stock
300ml (1/2 pint) milk
Salt
White pepper
2.5ml (1/2 teaspoon) castor sugar

## Method

1. Trim the discoloured leaves off the sprouts, wash them well, and let them stand in a basin of cold salted water for about an hour, then drain them.

2. Boil a saucepan of water and add 10ml (a dessertspoon) of salt for each 1.2 litres (quart) of water and boil the sprouts for 15–20 minutes. Drain well and squeeze out as much moisture as possible.

3. Put the sprouts into a mortar and pound them until quite smooth then rub them through a sieve.

4. Put this purée into a clean saucepan, gradually stir in the stock and season to taste with white pepper, salt and

14

2.5ml (half a teaspoon) of castor
sugar. Bring to the boil.

5. Rub the butter into the flour and stir
this into the soup.

6. Boil the milk in a separate saucepan,
and just before serving the soup add
the boiling milk to it.

7. Serve with small croutons of toasted
bread.

*I. Hourston, Kirkwall*

## Fish Soup

900g (2 lb) white
fish
300ml (½ pint)
shrimps
50g (2 oz) butter
600ml (1 pint)
milk
50g (2 oz) flour
1.8 litres
(3 pints) water
2 carrots
1 leek
½ stick of celery
Bunch of herbs
(bayleaf, thyme
and parsley)
Blade of mace
5ml (1 teaspoon)
chopped
parsley
Pepper and salt

*Method*

1. Chop the fish into pieces and put
them into a saucepan with 1.8 litres
(three pints) of cold water.

2. Add the vegetables thinly sliced, the
herbs and the mace. Bring to the
boil and skim.

3. Add the seasoning and boil for two
hours until the vegetables are quite
tender.

4. Strain as much of the soup as
possible through a sieve.

5. Melt the butter in a saucepan. Mix in
the flour, then gradually stir in the
milk. Stir constantly until it boils.

6. Return the soup to its saucepan, and
add the thickened milk, stirring until
it almost boils.

7. Just before serving, add the finely
chopped parsley and the shrimps.

*L. Flett, Orphir*

## Lobster Shell Soup

225g (1/2 lb)
  lobster shell
50g (2 oz) butter
1 whiting
  (cooked)
50g (2 oz) flour
1.2 litres
  (2 pints) stock
1 carrot
1 turnip
1 onion
Celery
Mace
Herbs and
  seasoning

### Method

1. Clean the lobster shell and pound with the butter until quite fine.

2. Put lobster shell and butter into a pan and heat to dissolve, then fry for a few minutes, adding flour.

3. Add stock, herbs, vegetables and whiting.

4. Boil for half an hour.

5. Add more stock if it is too thick.

6. Strain and reheat, adding a little cream.

7. Serve very hot.

**D. Laughton, Holm**

## Oxtail Soup

450g (1 lb) oxtail
2 onions
2 carrots
Turnip
10ml (1 dessert-
  spoon) vinegar
125ml (1 wine-
  glass) port
  wine
5ml
  (1 teaspoon)
  black pepper
Sweet herbs

### Method

1. Steep the oxtail in cold water for 2 hours.

2. Put the oxtail into water with the vegetables, sweet herbs and a teaspoon of black pepper.

3. Cover closely, and when it boils, skim off the fat.

4. Simmer for 3 hours.

5. Add the vinegar and port wine to serve.

**P. Tulloch, Kirkwall**

# Beef Brose

**Beef stock**
**Oatmeal**

## Method

1. After beef has been boiled and removed from the pot, skim off the fat with part of the liquor and boil it in a saucepan.

2. Toast a bowl of oatmeal before the fire until it is nicely browned.

3. Stir the liquor into the oatmeal until it is a good soup consistency.

4. Serve immediately.

*N. Kirk, Kirkwall*

# Lentil Soup

**225g (1/2 lb) brown lentils (soaked for 3 hours)**
**2 onions, chopped**
**2 carrots, chopped**
**50g (2 oz) streaky bacon**
**Bouquet garni**
**1.5 litres (2 1/2 pints) stock**
**Seasoning**

## Method

1. Dice the bacon and heat in a saucepan until the fat begins to run then add the onion and cook for 2–3 minutes.

2. Add the drained lentils, seasoning, carrot and stock, bring to the boil and put in the bouquet garni.

3. Simmer for 1–1 1/2 hours until the lentils are soft.

*E. Leslie, Kirkwall*

# Mutton Soup with Dumplings

675g (1½ lb)
  boiling mutton
2.4 litres
  (4 pints) water
225g (8 oz)
  yellow split
  peas (soaked
  overnight)
4 carrots, grated
2 onions,
  chopped
Salt and pepper

## Method

1. Boil the water, add the peas and mutton, simmer for one and a half hours, then skim.

2. Add the carrots, onions and seasoning and simmer for a further three quarters of an hour.

3. Add the dumplings and cook for 20 mins.

4. The mutton and dumplings are taken from the soup and served with vegetables as the second course.

## Dumplings

225g (8 oz) flour
15ml (1 table-
  spoon) sugar
2.5ml (½ tea-
  spoon) salt
2.5ml (½ tea-
  spoon) baking
  soda
Milk to mix

## Method

1. Mix all the ingredients with milk to form a dough.

2. Divide the mixture into four equal parts.

3. Roll well in flour and boil in soup for final 20 mins.

**M. Lyon, Stromness**

# FISH

## Smoked Fish Supreme

Small quantity
of butter
340g (12 oz)
smoked fish
600ml (2 cups)
milk
Crustless slices
of bread
110g (4 oz)
cheese, grated
2 eggs

### Method

1. Grease a 20cm (8-inch) pie dish with butter.

2. Cover bottom and sides with slices of buttered bread.

3. Break fish into chunks and place on top of bread.

4. Cover fish with cheese.

5. Beat eggs and milk together and pour over contents.

6. Bake for 45 minutes in oven (180°C, 350°F, gas mark 4).

*J. Butcher, South Ronaldsay*


## Birsay Haddock Soufflé

25g (1 oz)
margarine
25g (1 oz) flour
150ml (¼ pint)
milk
2 eggs,
separated
1 haddock,
boiled
Seasoning

### Method

1. Skin and bone haddock then rub through a sieve.

2. Melt margarine in a pan and add flour.

3. Slowly add milk to make a thick sauce.

4. Remove from heat, add egg yolks, fish and seasoning.

5. Fold in stiffly beaten whites.

6. Bake for 25–30 minutes in oven (180°C, 350°F, gas mark 4).

*B. Coghill, Birsay*

## Pentland Firth Pie

110g (¼ lb)
  cooked cod
225g (½ lb)
  mashed
  potatoes
10ml (1 dessert-
  spoon) butter
Salt and pepper

### Method

1. Skin, flake and remove bones from cod.

2. Melt butter in pan and add the potatoes—if too dry add 15ml (a tablespoon) of milk—and beat well with a fork.

3. Add the fish and season to taste. Heat thoroughly.

4. Put neatly into a pie dish and brown under the grill.

*T. Robertson, Longhope*

## Baked Stuffed Birsay Cod

1 medium cod
50g (2 oz) lard

**Stuffing**
30ml (2 table-
  spoons) bread-
  crumbs
15ml (1 table-
  spoon)
  chopped suet
10ml (½ table-
  spoon) parsley,
  chopped
1 egg to bind
Juice of 1 lemon
  with a little
  grated rind
Salt and pepper

**Coating**
Melted margarine and
  brown breadcrumbs

### Method

1. Wash fish and remove bones.

2. Prepare stuffing by mixing ingredients together and binding stiffly with beaten egg.

3. Press stuffing into centre of fish and tie into shape.

4. Brush with melted margarine and sprinkle with the breadcrumbs.

5. Place fish in melted lard in a baking tin and bake for 30 minutes in oven (180°C, 350°F, gas mark 4), basting frequently.

6. Serve on a hot ashet garnished with parsley.

*D. Taylor, Birsay*

# Casserole of Smoked Fish

450g (1 lb)
  smoked fillets
25g (1 oz)
  margarine
25g (1 oz) flour
300ml (1/2 pint)
  milk
150ml (1/4 pint)
  water
5ml (1 teaspoon)
  finely chopped
  onion
15ml (1 table-
  spoon) finely
  chopped ham
Pepper to taste

## Method

1. Place the milk, water, onion, ham, margarine and pepper in a pan. Cover and simmer for 10 minutes.

2. Wash the fillets and cut them into neat pieces. Add to the mixture in the pan and simmer for 30 minutes.

3. Mix the flour to a smooth paste with a little milk. Add this to the mixture and stir to boil.

4. Serve with mashed potatoes and thin fingers of toast.

*T. Foubister, Kirkwall*


# Baked Fillets with Tomato Sauce

8 fillets of sole
3 large tomatoes
1 onion
15ml (1 table-
  spoon) milk
Tomato sauce
Seasoning

## Method

1. Mix the chopped tomatoes and onion together.

2. Season the fillets, then spread the tomatoes and onion on them.

3. Fold the fillets over and place in a buttered baking dish with a tablespoon of milk, and bake in oven for 20 minutes (180°C, 350°F, gas mark 4).

4. Serve with tomato sauce.

*J. Leslie, Kirkwall*

# Fish Casserole

340g (³/₄ lb)
  white fish
  fillets
1 large onion
3 tomatoes
50g (2 oz)
  margarine
450ml (³/₄ pint)
  milk
Salt and pepper

## Method

1. Place fillets in a greased casserole dish.

2. Slice onions into rings and place on top of fish.

3. Slice tomatoes and add along with seasoning.

4. Pour on milk and dot with margarine.

5. Bake for one hour in oven (180°C, 350°F, gas mark 4). Scallops or clams may be used in place of fillets.

**M. Davidson, Balfour**


# Soused Herring

6 herrings
2 small onions,
  cut into rings
300ml (¹/₂ pint)
  mixed vinegar
  and water
15ml (1 table-
  spoon) mixed
  pickling spice
4 bay leaves
Salt and pepper

## Method

1. Scale, clean and bone herrings.

2. Season well with salt and pepper.

3. Roll up and place fairly close together in an ovenproof dish.

4. Cover with vinegar and water.

5. Sprinkle with pickling spice.

6. Garnish with bay leaves and onion rings.

7. Cover with baking foil or lid and bake for 45 minutes in oven (180°C, 350°F, gas mark 4).

**H. Garson, Sandwick**

# Orkney Seaside Curry

Limpets to fill a
  3.6 litre (6-pint)
  pot
10ml (2
  teaspoons)
  curry powder
50g (2 oz) fat
110g (4 oz) rice

## Method

1. Boil sufficient water to cover the limpets.

2. Add the limpets and boil until they come out of their shells.

3. Strain, cool and then remove the heads.

4. Mince limpets and fry in fat for a few minutes.

5. Add the curry powder and serve on bed of cooked rice.

**M. Mainland, Birsay**

# Devilled Lobsters

1 large lobster
5ml (1 teaspoon)
  chutney
25g (1 oz) butter
2.5ml (1/2 tea-
  spoon) mustard
5ml
  (1 teaspoon)
  Worcester
  sauce
45ml
  (3 tablespoons)
  white sauce
A dust of
  cayenne
Salt
Brown bread-
  crumbs

## Method

1. Take all the meat from a large boiled lobster and cut into small pieces.

2. Pound the coral in a mortar with the mustard, butter and other flavourings.

3. Put the white sauce (see p63) into a saucepan and add the pounded coral etc to it.

4. Let it heat thoroughly, then stir in the lobster and bring it to boiling point.

5. Prepare buttered fireproof shells on a dish. Put the mixture into these, and sprinkle the top with brown breadcrumbs. Brown under the grill.

6. Garnish with fresh parsley to serve.

**I. MacDonald, Kirkwall**

## Crofters' Hotpot

4 large herring
  fillets
50g (2 oz) butter
2 large onions,
  sliced
4 medium
  potatoes, sliced
Salt and pepper

### Method

1. Season fillets well and place half in a well-greased dish.

2. Cover fillets with onion slices then with potato slices.

3. Season and dab with butter.

4. Repeat layers, finishing with potatoes.

5. Season again and dab with butter.

6. Cover closely and bake for 50 minutes in oven (220°C, 425°F, gas mark 7). Remove cover and bake for another 10 minutes.

**Mrs Bleshe, Westray**

## Orkney Trout Crunch

1 trout
25g (1 oz) butter
25g (1 oz) flour
1 large can evap-
  orated milk
30ml (2 table-
  spoons) lemon
  juice
1/2 stick finely
  chopped celery
110g (4 oz)
  breadcrumbs
50g (2 oz)
  melted butter
Seasoning

### Method

1. Melt 25g (1 oz) butter in a pan and add flour.

2. Gradually stir in evaporated milk. Bring to the boil, stirring until thickened.

3. Flake trout, and add to sauce with lemon juice, celery and seasoning.

4. Mix well, and put into a greased 1.2-litre (2-pint) pie dish.

5. Mix breadcrumbs with melted butter and sprinkle on top.

6. Bake for 30 minutes in oven (180°C, 350°F, gas mark 4).

Alternatively, use a can of salmon.

**H. Garson, Sandwick**

# Salmon Pie

½ tin salmon
200ml (1 teacup) milk
200ml (1 teacup) breadcrumbs
50g (2 oz) margarine
2 eggs
Salt and pepper

## Method

1. Put milk and margarine into pan and heat slowly till margarine melts.

2. Add breadcrumbs.

3. Beat eggs.

4. Break up salmon with a fork.

5. Mix all ingredients together and put in a well-greased dish.

6. Bake for 30 minutes in oven (180°C, 350°F, gas mark 4).

7. Serve with chips, or cold with salad.

**J. Muir, Stenness**

# Graemsay Partan

1 boiled partan (large crab)
1 hard-boiled egg finely grated
30ml (2 tablespoons) fresh breadcrumbs
15ml (1 tablespoon) salad cream
Seasoning

## Method

1. Pick all the meat from the boiled partan, discarding the stomach bag.

2. Place the meat in a bowl and add the egg, breadcrumbs, salad cream, and seasoning.

3. Mix together, and place on a bed of lettuce, garnished with tomatoes.

4. Serve with oatcakes.

**M. Lyon, Stenness**

# Fricassée of Fish

450g (1 lb) white fish
1 shallot or small onion
600ml (1 pint) milk
2 hard-boiled eggs
25g (1 oz) butter
25g (1 oz) flour
Parsley
Salt
A blade of mace
Pinch of cayenne
6 drops lemon juice
Strip of lemon peel, 2.5cm (one inch)

## Method

1. Boil the milk in a stewpan with the shallot, mace, cayenne and lemon peel.

2. Cut the fish into pieces 4cm (1½ inches) square and simmer in the milk for 15 minutes. Remove the fish and keep it warm.

3. To prepare the sauce, melt the butter in a saucepan, add the flour, and fry without browning.

4. Strain the milk onto the butter, add a pinch of salt, and boil for 3 minutes stirring constantly.

5. Arrange the fish in the centre of a very hot dish. Take the sauce off the heat, add the lemon juice and pour it over the fish.

6. Cut the eggs into 8 pieces lengthways. Put 2 pieces on top of the fish with a sprig of parsley between, then form a border round the dish with the other pieces of egg, placing a sprig of parsley between each piece of egg.

*P. Laird, Kirkwall*

# MEAT

## Home-Brew Orkney Stew

450g (1 lb) lean
stewing steak
1 large kidney
225g (½ lb)
turnip
225g (½ lb) car-
rots
450g (1 lb) small
scrubbed new
potatoes
2 large onions
110g (¼ lb)
mushrooms
150ml (½ cup)
ground oatmeal
Home-brew ale
Bisto gravy
Seasoned flour

### Method

1. Heat a little oil in a stewing pan.

2. Roll pieces of meat and kidney in seasoned flour and seal in the hot oil.

3. Add sufficient home-brew ale to cover.

4. Bring to the boil and simmer gently for 75 minutes.

5. Add chopped carrots, turnip, onions and oatmeal. Return to the boil and simmer for another 15 minutes.

6. Add mushrooms and Bisto gravy and simmer for another 8 minutes before serving.

*I. Thomson, Stromness*

## Beefsteak and Kidney Pudding

900g (2 lb) steak
675g (1½ lb)
suet paste
1 ox kidney
1 shallot
Vinegar
5ml (1 teaspoon)
parsley
Salt
Pepper

### Method

1. Cut the beefsteak into pieces.

2. Cover the kidney with cold water, add a tablespoon of vinegar and let it soak for 10 minutes. Rinse it in cold water, dry it, core it and slice it.

3. Butter a pudding basin and line it with suet paste leaving a good margin hanging over the edge.

4. Put in a layer of the steak and kidney, sprinkle it with a little of the chopped parsley, shallot, pepper and salt. Repeat the layers until the basin is full, then pour in 150ml (half a cup) of cold water.

5. Cut out a piece of paste the size of the basin and lay it on top. Wet the edges, fold over the margin of paste lining and press down firmly.

6. Lay a buttered paper over the top, then a pudding cloth and tie it on firmly.

7. Put the pudding in a saucepan partly filled with boiling water and boil for 4 hours.

8. Turn the pudding out on to a hot dish and garnish with a little chopped parsley to serve.

*B. Muir, Stromness*

## Stewed Steak and Oysters

675g (1½ lb) steak
18 oysters
50g (2 oz) butter
1 onion
60ml (½ wineglass) Port wine
5ml (1 teaspoon) flour
300ml (½ pint) water
Pepper and salt

### Method

1. Melt the butter in a stewpan. Slice the onion and fry it in the butter until it is golden brown.

2. Cut the steak into thick pieces and fry in the butter for 15 minutes.

3. Add the water and season to taste.

4. Add the liquor from the oysters, cover the pan, and let it simmer for 1 hour.

5. Mix the flour with the port wine and thicken the gravy.

6. Draw the pan from the heat, add the oysters and stir until they are plump. Do not let it boil.

7. Dish up the steak, put the oysters round, and pour on the gravy.

8. Garnish with croutons of fried bread, brushed with white of egg and dipped in grated parmesan cheese.

*J. Leslie, Kirkwall*

## Beef Olives

Long thin steaks
125ml (1 glass)
  white wine
Brown gravy
Cayenne
Oil
Flour
Butter

*Forcemeat*
Breadcrumbs
Beef suet,
  minced
Parsley, chopped
Egg yolk
Grated lemon
  peel
Nutmeg
Salt and pepper

### Method

1. Mix all the ingredients together to prepare the forcemeat.

2. Spread a layer of the forcemeat over each steak, roll and tie with fine string.

3. Fry the olives lightly in oil, then add gravy, wine and a little cayenne. Thicken with a little flour and butter.

4. Cover tightly and stew for 1 hour. Remove string to serve.

**P. Tulloch, Kirkwall**

## Baked Beef and Bacon Loaf

110g (4 oz)
  bacon, minced
225g (8 oz) raw
  beef, minced
110g (4 oz)
  white bread-
  crumbs
1 onion
5ml (1 teaspoon)
  mixed herbs
A little stock
Salt and pepper

### Method

1. Mix bacon, beef and breadcrumbs together.

2. Finely chop onion and add to beef mixture with herbs and seasoning.

3. Moisten with a little stock and put into a greased loaf tin.

4. Cover with foil and bake for 2 hours in oven (180°C, 350°F, gas mark 4).

5. Serve with jacket potatoes.

**M. Tulloch, Sanday**

## Balfour Beef

900g (2 lb) beef
450g (1 lb)
  bacon
1 lemon rind
2 egg yolks
2.5ml (1/2 tea-
  spoon) nutmeg
Pepper and salt
Thyme and
  parsley
Brown gravy
Fried potatoes

### Method

1. Chop the beef finely, pass the bacon through the mincer twice and mix them together.

2. Finely chop the lemon rind and mix it with the parsley and thyme. Add the grated nutmeg and pepper and salt to taste. The quantity of salt must be according to the saltiness of the bacon.

3. Add all these ingredients to the chopped meat and mix them together with the egg yolks.

4. Form the mixture into a roll and wrap it in buttered paper and bind it with tape to keep it in shape. Put it in a well-greased baking tin, and bake in oven for 1–1½ hours (180°C, 350°F, gas mark 4).

5. When cooked, remove the binding and paper, place the roll on a hot dish and pour on a rich brown gravy.

6. Garnish with fried potatoes to serve.

*E. Miller, Kirkwall*

## Ward Speciality

450g (1 lb) stew-
  ing steak, in a
  lump
2 onions
1 curry stock
  cube
Shake of chilli
  powder
4 carrots
340g (12 oz) rice
Oil

### Method

1. Slice the steak very thinly and cut roughly into 5 cm x 2.5 cm (2" x 1") pieces.

2. Fry quickly in the oil, browning the pieces thoroughly.

3. Add the onion, diced, and brown slightly.

4. Dissolve the stock cube in 150–300ml

(1/4–1/2 pint) of water and add to frying pan along with seasoning, chilli and sliced carrots, and allow to simmer till carrots are cooked.

5. Serve on a bed of boiled rice.

*L. Ward, Sanday*

## *Mutton Cutlets with Tomatoes*

**6 mutton cutlets**
**8 medium toma-**
  **toes**
**Mashed potatoes**
**Butter**
**Pepper**
**Salt**

*Method*

1. Cut the cutlets from the best end of a neck of mutton. Trim them neatly and scrape the end bone.

2. Put some butter on a plate and season it well with pepper and salt. Dip the cutlets in the seasoned butter and let them soak for an hour.

3. Submerge the tomatoes in boiling water and then skin them. Put them into a buttered baking dish, season with pepper, salt and a pinch of castor sugar. Lay a buttered paper over them to cook in oven for 15–20 minutes (180°C, 350°F, gas mark 4).

4. Lay the cutlets on a grill and cook quickly.

5. Prepare mashed potatoes and arrange a straight line down the centre of a dish.

6. Place the cutlets down the centre of the potatoes letting one cutlet overlap another.

7. Arrange a border of tomatoes down each side.

*P. Harcus, Kirkwall*

## Gairsay Mutton

450g (1 lb) mutton
25g (1 oz) flour
Spaghetti
25g (1 oz) butter
8 button onions
2 small young carrots
1 small turnip
1 tomato
Herbs
600ml (1 pint) weak stock or water
Pepper
Salt

## Method

1. Cut the mutton into small pieces.

2. Melt the butter in a stewpan, then put in the meat, the onions and the sliced carrots and turnip. Fry until a golden colour, then stir in the flour.

3. Add the stock or water, pepper and salt to taste, and a bunch of savoury herbs tied up in muslin. Bring to the boil and skim well.

4. Reduce the heat, and simmer for 1–1½ hours.

5. Boil spaghetti in salted water with an onion, and make a border of it round the dish. Pour the ragout into the centre.

6. Arrange a twist of spaghetti on the top and serve.

**T. Mowat, Kirkwall**

## Mutton Fritters

450g (1 lb) breast of mutton
1 carrot
1 small turnip
½ stick of celery
1 large onion
Frying batter
Frying fat
A bunch of herbs (bayleaf, thyme and parsley)
Pepper and salt

## Method

1. Clean and slice the vegetables and put them into a saucepan with the meat. Cover with cold water, bring to the boil and remove scum.

2. Simmer gently until the meat is tender.

3. Take the meat from the saucepan and lay it on a flat plate, sprinkle it with finely chopped parsley, onion and salt and pepper.

4. Put another flat dish on top with a weight on it and allow to stand until the meat is cold.

5. Cut the meat into fingers 5 cm by 4 cm (2 inches by 1½ inches), dip them in frying batter and fry in hot fat until they are golden brown.

6. Arrange neatly on a hot dish and sprinkle a little chopped parsley on the top. Pour on Reform sauce (see p66) to serve.

*E. Miller, Kirkwall*

## Stewed Breast of Lamb

A breast of lamb
White stock
50g (2 oz) butter
75g (3 oz) flour
900ml (1½ pints) green peas
Potato balls
1 blade of mace
5ml (1 teaspoon) salt
2.5ml (½ teaspoon) white pepper

*Method*

1. Cut the lamb into pieces and lay in a stewpan with a blade of mace, and sprinkle with 5ml (a teaspoon) of salt and 2.5ml (½ teaspoon) of white pepper.

2. Add stock to cover, place the lid on the pan and simmer gently for 45 minutes. Skim well and remove the mace.

3. Add 600ml (1 pint) of the peas and simmer for another 30 minutes.

4. Mix the butter and flour together and stir it into the gravy. Simmer for another 10 minutes.

5. Take out the pieces of meat and arrange on a dish. Pour on the sauce, garnish with potato balls, and the remaining 300ml (½ pint) of peas, plainly boiled.

*B. Muir, Stromness*

## Peedie Pies

450g (1 lb) lean
 mutton
1 onion
110g (1/4 lb)
 mushrooms
Seasoning
Flour to thicken
340g (3/4 lb)
 short crust
 pastry

*Method*

1. Chop the mutton, mushrooms and onion into small pieces.

2. Put the chopped mutton into a pan with sufficient water to cover and cook until tender.

3. Add the mushrooms and onion to the pan, season and cook for another ten minutes.

4. Thicken with flour and allow to cool.

5. Roll out the pastry and cut into rounds to line small bun tins, retaining enough pastry to make rounds to cover.

6. Spoon some of the mixture into each pastry case.

7. Cut a small hole in the centre of each pastry lid, place them in position and seal the edges.

8. Brush with egg, and bake until brown.

*J. Watt, Stromness*

## Baked Orkney Ham with Bananas

3 slices Orkney
 ham 2cm (3/4")
 thick
3 bananas, sliced
150ml (1/2 cup)
 brown sugar
150ml (1/2 cup)
 flaked coconut
60ml (4 table-
 spoons) lemon
 juice
30ml (2 table-
 spoons) butter

*Method*

1. Cut the ham slices in half.

2. Arrange in a shallow greased baking tin and spread sliced bananas on top.

3. Sprinkle on the lemon juice, brown sugar and coconut.

4. Bake for 1 hour in oven (180°C, 350°F, gas mark 4).

*J. Flett, Orphir*

34

# Stenness Ham and Tomato Pie

140g (5 oz) shortcrust pastry
225g (1/2 lb) ham
2 small tomatoes
1 boiled potato
1 hard-boiled egg
50g (2 oz) Orkney cheese, grated
150ml (1/4 pint) milk
1 egg
Salt and pepper

## Method

1. Line a dish with half the pastry.

2. Beat the egg with the milk and seasoning.

3. Chop ham, tomatoes, potato, and hard-boiled egg and place in dish, topped with grated cheese.

4. Pour in egg mixture and cover with other half of pastry.

5. Bake for 10 minutes in oven (190°C, 375°F, gas mark 5), then lower heat and continue cooking for a further 30 minutes.

*W. Reid, Stenness*

# Baked Sweetbreads

1 calf's sweetbread
1 beaten egg
Breadcrumbs
Gravy
Salt
25g (1 oz) butter

## Method

1. Boil the sweetbread for 15 minutes in slightly salted water. Dry it, then cut it in half lengthwise.

2. Dip each half into the beaten egg, then into fine white breadcrumbs.

3. Butter a baking tin, lay the pieces in and bake in oven for 20 minutes (180°C, 350°F, gas mark 4), basting them with the butter.

4. Lay the pieces side by side on a hot dish, pour on a brown gravy, and garnish with fried parsley to serve.

*L. Grieve, Kirkwall*

## Stronsay Veal

675g (1½ lbs)
cooked veal
225g (½ lb)
cooked ham
2 onions
1 egg
Nutmeg
Pepper and salt
Butter
Sauce
One thick slice of
bread
Milk

## Method

1. Chop the veal and ham very finely.

2. Soak the bread in some milk.

3. Melt a little butter in a stewpan and fry the chopped onion until slightly brown.

4. Mix in the meat and the bread.

5. Add a large pinch of grated nutmeg, pepper and salt to taste. Stir until thoroughly mixed and heated.

6. Take the pan from the heat and stir in a well-beaten egg.

7. Butter a mould, press the mixture firmly in and bake in a moderate oven for 1 hour.

8. Turn it out and serve with German sauce (see p66).

*I. MacDonald, Kirkwall*

# POULTRY AND GAME

## Country-style Chicken

1 chicken
1 onion
1 clove garlic
50g (2 oz) diced bacon
50g (2 oz) butter
50g (2 oz) flour
900ml (1½ pints) stock
4 peeled and chopped tomatoes
½ tin chopped pineapple
1 small tin button mushrooms
2.5ml (½ teaspoon) sage
Salt and pepper

### Method

1. Cut chicken into 4 joints and brown in a pan with the butter and the clove of garlic.

2. Add the onion and bacon and fry lightly.

3. Sprinkle with flour and stir well.

4. Add the sage and seasoning then the stock. Cover with a lid, and cook gently for 25 minutes.

5. Just before cooked, add the tomatoes, the mushrooms, and the pineapple, with a little of the juice.

6. Serve with pieces of fried bread and potatoes.

*H. Garson, Sandwick*

## Chicken stuffed with Mushrooms

2 small spring chickens
110g (4 oz) mushrooms
110g (4 oz) butter
1 onion
75g (3 oz) single cream
5ml (1 teaspoon) cornflour
Chopped parsley
Paprika

### Method

1. Finely chop the onion and cook in half the butter for 5 minutes with the lid on the pan. Slice the mushrooms, add to the onions and cook for 4 minutes. Season and allow to cool.

2. Stuff the chickens with the mushroom mixture. Melt the rest of the butter in a fireproof dish and gently fry the chickens until brown. Season well, and pour over 30ml

37

(2 tablespoons) of water. Cook in oven for 20 minutes (180°C, 350°F, gas mark 4).

3. When tender, remove from the casserole and split each bird in half. Arrange on a warm serving dish and put in a low oven while you prepare the sauce.

4. To make the sauce, mix the cream with the gravy in the casserole, bring slowly to the boil and season to taste. Add 30ml (2 tablespoons) of cornflour to thicken.

5. Spoon the sauce over each bird and decorate with chopped parsley to serve.

*T. Bews, Kirkwall*

## Oyster Chicken

1 chicken
12 oysters
600ml (1 pint) gravy
2 blades of mace
1/2 sliced nutmeg
Sweet herbs
110g (1/4 lb) butter
Flour
Seasoning
1 anchovy
60ml (1/2 glass) white wine
1/2 lemon

### Method

1. Part-boil the chicken and cut the meat into small pieces. Stew in the gravy with the oysters, mace, nutmeg, herbs and seasoning.

2. When nearly done, take out the herbs, mace and nutmeg.

3. Add the butter, flour, chopped anchovy and wine.

4. Garnish with sliced lemon to serve.

*K. Wilson, Stromness*

# Chicken Baked in Rice

1 chicken
Slices of ham
600ml (1 pint) gravy
1 onion, finely minced
Boiled rice
Flour paste
Seasoning

## Method

1. Line a pudding dish with slices of ham.

2. Cut the chicken into joints, season well, and lay them in the pudding dish.

3. Add the gravy and onion.

4. Fill the dish with boiled rice, well pressed and piled as high as possible.

5. Cover with a paste of flour and water and bake for 1 hour.

6. Remove the paste to serve.

**J. Thomson, Stromness**

# Smothered Turkey

8 large slices cold turkey
340g (3/4 lb) rice
75g (1 1/2 oz) butter
1 onion, finely chopped
300ml (1/2 pint) soured cream
Pinch of nutmeg
30ml (2 table-spoons) chopped chives
Seasoning

## Method

1. Cook the rice in boiling salted water. Drain and rinse with hot water. Dry and put in the bottom of casserole dish.

2. Cover the rice with the slices of turkey. Cover with buttered paper and heat in oven for 20 minutes.

3. Melt the butter, and cook the finely chopped onion until tender but not brown. Add the soured cream, seasoning, and the pinch of nutmeg and mix well.

4. Spoon the soured cream sauce over the turkey and rice and sprinkle with chopped chives to serve.

**J. Brown, Stromness**

# Rabbit Hotpot

1 rabbit
110g (¼ lb)
  streaky bacon
4 onions
Small head of
  celery
Small white
  cabbage
6 potatoes
Stock or water
Flour
Pepper
Salt
125ml (1 glass)
  of red wine

## Method

1. Divide the rabbit into joints. Dip the pieces into seasoned flour and brown in a frying-pan.

2. Place the rabbit in a casserole draped with the bacon.

3. Prepare and slice the vegetables and place around the rabbit.

4. Half fill the casserole with stock or water, pour on the wine and season well. Cover and cook in oven for 2½ hours (180°C, 350°F, gas mark 4).

*L. Cooper, Kirkwall*

# Duck with Red Cabbage

1 medium duck
1 small red
  cabbage
3 onions
30ml (2 table-
  spoons) vinegar
30ml (2 table-
  spoons) water
4 cooking apples
5ml (1 teaspoon)
  sugar
30ml (2 table-
  spoons) oil
5ml (1 teaspoon)
  caraway seeds
150ml (¼ pint)
  stock
15ml (1 table-
  spoon) chopped
  parsley

## Method

1. Braise the cabbage, then shred it very finely. Chop up one of the onions and mix it with the cabbage then place it in a well-buttered casserole. Add vinegar, water and seasoning. Cover, and cook in oven for 1 hour (180°C, 350°F, gas mark 4). Add the sliced apples with a little sugar, and cook for another 15 minutes.

2. Cut the duck into 4 pieces. Heat the oil, and brown the pieces of duck all over. Now place the duck on top of the cabbage in the casserole.

3. Cook the 2 remaining sliced onions in the remaining oil until just soft. Sprinkle in the caraway seeds and add a little stock. Add seasoning, and pour over the pieces of duck.

Return to the oven for 40 minutes until tender.

4. Scrape the onion mixture off the duck and mix well into the cabbage. Arrange the pieces of duck on top of the cabbage and sprinkle with chopped parsley.

5. Serve hot with mashed potatoes and redcurrant jelly.

*N. Bruce, Kirkwall*

## Pigeons with Rice and Parmesan Cheese

3 pigeons
Butter
Flour
1.2 litres
   (2 pints) stock
2 onions, grated
Seasoning
1 egg, beaten
Juice of 1 lemon
225g (1/2 lb) rice
Nutmeg, grated
Salt
150ml (1/2 cup)
   grated
   Parmesan
   cheese

### Method

1. Clean the pigeons and cut them into quarters.

2. Brown some of the butter with flour and add 600ml (1 pint) of stock, the grated onions and seasoning. Stew the pigeons until tender.

3. Take out the pigeons and add the lemon juice to the stock, bring to the boil, and strain over the pigeons.

4. Boil the rice in 600ml (1 pint) of stock with a knob of butter, some grated nutmeg and salt. When the rice is cooked, dry it and add half the Parmesan cheese.

5. Put half the rice round the dish, place the pigeons in the dish and cover with the remains of the rice. Pour over the egg, and sprinkle over the rest of the cheese.

6. Bake for 45 minutes in oven (150°C, 300°F, gas mark 2). It should be a fine golden colour when ready.

*W. Tait, Kirkwall*

## Wardhill Pie

1 rabbit
1 onion
50g (2 oz) grated raw potato
50g (2 oz) suet
225g (8 oz) flour
15ml (1 tablespoon) baking powder
Salt and pepper

### Method

1. Wash the rabbit in salted water and cut into neat joints.

2. Mix the flour with the baking powder, salt and suet.

3. Add the grated potato and mix to a dry dough with very little water.

4. Roll out thinly, & use two thirds of the dough to line a greased pudding bowl.

5. Put the rabbit into the bowl with the onion, a few diced potatoes and seasoning.

6. Add a little stock and cover with remaining pastry dough.

7. Cover with greaseproof paper and steam for 2 hours.

*T. Robertson, Longhope*

## Game Pie

2 grouse
225g (1/2 lb) steak
225g (1/2 lb) streaky bacon
1 large onion
6 mushrooms
30ml (2 tablespoons) chopped herbs
300ml (1/2 pint) red wine
300ml (1/2 pint) stock
1 egg
Puff pastry
Pinch of nutmeg
Seasoning

### Method

1. Cut the meat off the grouse, cut the steak and bacon into small pieces. Arrange in a pie-dish in layers with finely chopped onion, mushrooms, herbs and seasoning between each layer.

2. Pour on the red wine and enough stock to barely cover the meat. Cover with foil and bake slowly in oven for 1–1½ hours (160°C, 325°F, gas mark 3) until the meat is tender. Allow to cool.

3. Roll out the pastry, cut a strip, moisten it, and place it round the edge of the dish. Moisten the top of

the strip, and place a large piece of pastry on top and press the edges together. Cut off any surplus and crimp the edges. Slash the top of the pastry to release steam and decorate with pastry leaves.

4. Bake in oven for 30 minutes (220°C, 425°F, gas mark 7).

*J. Chalmers, Stromness*

## Turkey Cutlets

170g (6 oz) turkey
25g (1 oz) butter
1 onion, chopped
170g (6 oz) mashed potatoes
5ml (1 teaspoon) mixed herbs
30ml (2 table-spoons) chut-ney
Tomato sauce
1 egg
50g (2 oz) flour
2 eggs beaten with 5ml (1 teaspoon) oil
170g (6 oz) white bread-crumbs
Fat to fry

### Method

1. Chop the turkey. Melt the butter and cook the onion until tender.

2. Add the onion to the turkey with enough mashed potato to make a firm mixture, stirring in the herbs, chutney, beaten egg and seasoning.

3. Mould the mixture into cutlet shapes, and roll in seasoned flour. Brush with eggs beaten in oil and cover with dry breadcrumbs.

4. Heat fat and fry cutlets for a few minutes until golden brown, drain and serve with tomato sauce.

*E. Johnston, Stromness*

# Rabbit with Mustard Sauce

2 rabbits
Seasoned flour
50g (2 oz) butter
110g (¼ lb)
 streaky bacon,
 chopped
2 large onions,
 chopped
5ml (1 teaspoon)
 dried herbs
150ml (¼ pint)
 dry white wine
150ml (¼ pint)
 stock
20ml (4 tea-
 spoons) Scotch
 mustard
300ml (½ pint)
 double Orkney
 cream

## Method

1. Joint the rabbits and coat with seasoned flour. Brown with the bacon in the melted butter.

2. Add the onions, herbs, wine and stock. Simmer gently until tender.

3. Strain the stock from the rabbit and keep the pieces warm in the oven in a serving dish.

4. Thoroughly mix the mustard into the fresh cream, add to the stock and season to taste.

5. Pour the sauce over the rabbit pieces to serve.

*P. Anderson, Kirkwall*

# Turkey and Asparagus

450ml
 (1½ cups)
 diced turkey
300ml (1 cup)
 hot white sauce
450ml
 (1½ cups) hot
 boiled rice
1 tin asparagus
75ml (¼ cup)
 mayonnaise

## Method

1. Chop the asparagus into 2.5 cm (1-inch) pieces.

2. Grease a shallow casserole dish and arrange half the turkey in a layer. Cover with the asparagus and top with the rest of the turkey.

3. Stir the mayonnaise into the white sauce (see p63), allow it to cool, then spoon it over the turkey. Bake uncovered in a hot oven for 20–30 minutes. Serve with rice.

# SAVOURY

## North Isles Savoury

4 hard-boiled
eggs
450g (1 lb) cold
boiled potatoes
Chopped chives
600ml (1 pint) of
white sauce
75g (3 oz) grated
cheese

### Method

1. Slice the eggs and potatoes and arrange in layers in an ovenproof dish.

2. Sprinkle each layer with chives.

3. Pour white sauce (see p63) over the last layer and cover the top with grated cheese.

4. Bake for 20 minutes in oven (200°C, 400°F, gas mark 6).

*R. Wallace, Shapinsay*

## Lyonnaise Eggs

6 eggs
450ml (1$^1/_2$ cups)
milk
1 chopped onion
1 tablespoon
flour
150ml ($^1/_2$ cup)
breadcrumbs
30ml (2 table-
spoons) butter
Salt and pepper

### Method

1. Cook the onion in the butter for 10 minutes. Add the flour, and cook until the mixture is smooth, stirring constantly.

2. Gradually pour in the milk, and cook for 3 minutes, stirring constantly.

3. Season with pepper and salt, and pour into a deep, hot baking dish.

4. Carefully break the 6 eggs into the mixture. Cover the eggs with the breadcrumbs.

5. Bake in oven for 10 minutes (180°C, 350°F, gas mark 4).

*E. Harvey, Stromness*

## Toasted Giants

450g (1 lb) pota-
toes, boiled
4 eggs, hard
boiled
2 medium
onions,
chopped
3 slices white
bread
300ml (½ pint)
white sauce
25g (1 oz) white
breadcrumbs
Seasoning

*Method*

1. Slice potatoes and eggs, and arrange in layers in a round, shallow pyrex dish and season well.

2. Stir chopped onions into hot, white sauce and add seasoning.

3. Pour the onion sauce over the egg and potato and sprinkle with breadcrumbs.

4. Bake for 30 minutes in oven (180°C, 350°F, gas mark 4) until golden brown.

5. Cut each slice of bread in half and toast lightly.

6. Cut the toasted pieces into the shape of standing stones and stand upright round the dish to serve.

*G. Sinclair, Stromness*

## Winter Supper

675g (1½ lbs)
potatoes
1 large Spanish
onion, chopped
220g (8 oz) can
of peeled
tomatoes
3 slices corned
beef
110g (4 oz)
Orkney cheese,
grated
50g (2 oz)
Orkney butter
Seasoning

*Method*

1. Boil potatoes and mash with butter.

2. Fry the onion in a little oil until light brown.

3. Strain the tomatoes and discard the juice. Add the tomatoes to the onions in the frying pan, and mix to heat.

4. Arrange layers in deep oven dish, potato, cheese, corned beef, onion, tomato, finishing with potato, with cheese sprinkled on top.

5. Bake for 20 minutes in oven (180°C, 350°F, gas mark 4).

*J. Leslie, Kirkwall*

# Ham Toast

120ml (8 table-
spoons) lean
ham
2 egg yolks
90ml (6 table-
spoons) cream
Butter
Cayenne
Toast

## Method

1. Take the lean remains of a ham, and chop finely.

2. To 120ml (8 tablespoons) of ham add the yolks of 2 eggs well beaten, the cream, a piece of butter about the size of an egg, and a seasoning of cayenne pepper.

3. Stir over a moderate heat until the mixture begins to thicken.

4. Spread on squares of toast and serve very hot.

**L. Flett, Orphir**

# Maeshowe Bacon Savoury

450g (1 lb) leeks,
sliced
1 can baked
beans
8 rashers bacon
110g (1/4 lb)
brussels
sprouts
110g (1/4 lb)
mushrooms
2 hard-boiled
eggs
1 tomato
Butter for frying

## Method

1. Fry the bacon rashers and keep hot in a dish.

2. Melt butter in the pan, add leeks and mushrooms, and fry until tender. Keep them hot in a dish.

3. Stir baked beans into fat in pan and heat well.

4. Boil the brussels sprouts.

5. To serve, heap the beans into the middle of a serving dish and top with sprouts rolled up in rashers of bacon. Heap leeks and mushrooms all around.

6. Garnish with slices or wedges of egg and fried tomato.

**L. Mathers, Stenness**

# Potato and Cheese Mould

225g (½ lb) cooked potatoes
50g (2 oz) grated cheese
30 ml (2 tablespoons) milk or cream
25g (1 oz) melted butter
2 eggs, separated
A few browned breadcrumbs
Pepper and salt

## Method

1. Sieve the potatoes and add the melted butter, the yolks of the eggs, the cheese, seasoning, and the milk or cream.

2. Whip the whites to a stiff froth and stir them lightly into the mixture.

3. Grease a mould or bowl, and line it with the breadcrumbs.

4. Pour in the mixture and bake for 30 minutes in oven (180°C, 350°F, gas mark 4).

5. Turn out on to a hot dish to serve.

**F. Kent, Westray**

# Cheese, Onion and Potato Pie

225g (8 oz) potatoes
½ an onion
75g (3 oz) cheese
25g (1 oz) margarine
75 ml (2½ fluid oz) milk
Salt and pepper
Chopped parsley
4 eggs

## Method

1. Boil potatoes.

2. Chop onion finely and fry until golden brown using half the margarine.

3. Drain the potatoes, add salt, pepper, milk, and the rest of the margarine and mash well.

4. Add the onion, a little parsley, and all but 30 ml (2 tablespoons) of the cheese. Mix well and place in a warm, ovenproof dish.

5. Make 4 hollows in the mixture with the back of a spoon.

6. Drop an egg into each hollow and put a dot of butter on top of each one.

7. Sprinkle the grated cheese between the eggs.

8. Bake for 15 minutes in oven (190°C, 375°F, gas mark 5) until the eggs set.

*J. Sinclair, Sanday*

## Stuffed Bacon on Toast

150ml (½ cup) dry bread-crumbs
Lamb's kidney
Beaten egg
10 slices bacon
½ small onion, chopped
10ml (½ table-spoon) parsley
Salt
Pepper

### Method

1. Mix the crumbs with the chopped onion, add parsley and seasoning, moisten with beaten egg, then spread the mixture on slices of bacon.

2. Fasten each slice round a piece of lamb's kidney with small skewers.

3. Bake in oven for 20 minutes (190°C, 375°F, gas mark 5).

4. Serve on rounds of hot toast with the crusts removed. Garnish with halved tomatoes, baked or grilled, sprinkled with breadcrumbs, pepper and salt, and dabs of butter.

*J. Flett, Kirkwall*

## Hamnavoe Pie

110g (4 oz) shortcrust pastry
110g (4 oz) cooked chicken
50g (2 oz) gam-mon
110g (4 oz) chopped mush-room
2 eggs
Salt and pepper

### Method

1. Line a 20cm (8-inch) sandwich tin with the pastry.

2. Chop the chicken and gammon and lay in the pastry.

3. Sprinkle the mushroom over the top.

4. Beat the eggs, season and pour over the mixture.

5. Bake in oven for 20 minutes (180°C, 350°F, gas mark 4) until eggs are set.

*Oakleigh Hotel, Stromness*

# Orkney Bacon Savoury

225g (½ lb)
bacon, minced
110g (¼ lb)
mushrooms,
chopped
3 tomatoes,
sliced
1 onion, chopped
2 beaten eggs
225g (½ lb)
grated cheese
110g (4 oz)
breadcrumbs
50g (2 oz)
margarine

## Method

1. Add the minced bacon and chopped onion to the beaten egg and beat again.

2. Mix the cheese and breadcrumbs together.

3. Grease a casserole and put in layers, half the bacon mixture, half the mushrooms, half the tomatoes, and half the cheese and breadcrumbs mixture.

4. Repeat the layers again in the same order.

5. Put dabs of margarine on the top and bake for 30 minutes in oven (200°C, 400°F, gas mark 6).

*E. Slater, Kirkwall*


# Scotch Nips

170g (6 oz)
cooked dried
haddock
2 egg yolks
15ml (1 table-
spoon) double
cream
White pepper
and salt

## Method

1. Chop up the fish and place it in a stew-pan.

2. Add the cream, egg yolks, pepper and salt to taste, and stir over a moderate heat till the mixture thickens.

3. Pile it on fried croutes, sprinkle with a little paprika and serve hot.

*J. Flett, Kirkwall*

# Cheesy Macaroni

225g (½ lb)
macaroni
340g (¾ lb)
mince
50g (2 oz) toma-
to purée
110g (4 oz) grat-
ed cheese
1 onion, finely
chopped
1 packet tomato
soup

## Method

1. Cook the mince and onion.

2. Add the tomato purée.

3. Make the soup using only half the quantity of water recommended then add this to the mince.

4. Cook the macaroni.

5. Grease a dish and layer the mince and macaroni until all the ingredients are used, ending with a layer of macaroni.

6. Sprinkle the grated cheese on top.

7. Bake for 20 minutes in oven (180°C, 350°F, gas mark 4) then brown under the grill.

**M. Butcher, South Ronaldsay**

# Rice with Cheese Sauce

1.2 litres (2
pints) boiled
rice
75ml (¼ cup)
grated Orkney
cheese
110g (¼ lb)
chopped fried
mushrooms
300ml (½ pint)
white sauce
Paprika to taste

## Method

1. Boil the rice in salted water. Drain well, then rinse it under the cold tap in a colander. Drain well and add it to the white sauce (see p63).

2. Season to taste with paprika, add the cheese and the mushrooms and heat until the cheese has melted, stirring lightly. Serve at once.

**L. Flett, Orphir**

## Kippered Eggs

2 kippers
25g (1 oz)
  margarine
30ml (2 table-
  spoons) milk
2 eggs
Salt and pepper
Buttered toast

### Method

1. Boil the kippers until tender.

2. When cold, remove the bones and flake the flesh.

3. Put into pan with margarine, milk, and lightly beaten eggs. Season lightly.

4. Cook gently, stirring constantly until eggs thicken.

5. Serve on buttered toast.

**H. Garson, Sandwick**


## Haddock Kedgeree

2 smoked
  haddocks
225g (8 oz)
  boiled rice
110g (4 oz)
  butter
2 hard-boiled
  eggs
Cayenne pepper
A few chopped
  mushrooms

### Method

1. Melt the butter in a pan and cook the mushrooms. Add the flaked fish, rice and pepper and heat thoroughly.

2. Serve garnished with rings of egg white and the chopped yolks sprinkled over the top.

**N. Wylie, Kirkwall**

# Stuffed Cabbage

1 small cabbage
110g (4 oz) lard
1 onion
900ml (3 cups)
  porage oats
Salt and pepper
Knob of butter

## Method

1. Keep the outside leaves of the cabbage but shred the rest of it.
2. Cut up onion and brown in fat.
3. When the onion is brown, add the oats, salt and pepper, and fry until brown.
4. Grease steamer and put butter in the bottom.
5. Put oat mixture in steamer in layers with shredded cabbage.
6. Cover with cabbage leaves and steam for 1–1½ hours.

**L. Mathers, Stenness**

# Trout Toast

A plump trout
White sauce
Lemon juice
Seasoning
Cream
Raw onion

## Method

1. Boil the trout and flake the flesh into a bowl.
2. Make a little white sauce (see p63), add the flaked fish and season to taste. A little lemon juice may be added if desired.
3. Add 15ml (a tablespoon) of cream, mix well, and serve on hot buttered wholemeal bread garnished with a sprinkling of chopped raw onion.

**L. Grieve, Kirkwall**

# Orkney Cheese

4.8 litres
 (8 pints) full
 cream milk
5ml
 (1 teaspoon) of
 rennet

## Method

1. Heat the milk till lukewarm (about 30°C, 85°F).

2. Add the rennet with a little cold water and stir for a few minutes.

3. Let it stand for about 30 minutes until it becomes a firm curd, then break it up with a knife.

4. Repeat the procedure then strain through muslin.

5. Gently break up the curd with your fingers, add a little salt, and mix well.

6. Place the cheese in a chessit (cheese press) with a cloth underneath and a cloth on top. Place the lid in position and put on a 3kg (7 lb) weight.

7. Take the cheese out and turn it for the next 8 days. Replace with a clean cloth each time.

8. Increase the weight after the first 2 days.

9. After the pressing is complete, dry it off at an open window.

**F. Marian McNeill**

# VEGETABLES AND SALADS

## Carrots in Lemon Butter

450g (1 lb)
  carrots
Butter
1/2 lemon
Salt

*Method*

1. Cut carrots into 7.5cm (3-inch) lengths, quarter, and chop into pieces about a quarter of an inch thick.

2. Melt a large knob of butter in a saucepan and add the juice of half a lemon.

3. Simmer the carrots for 10 minutes.

4. Drain on kitchen towel and serve crisp.

**E. Shaw, Kirkwall**

## New Carrots and Cream

1 bundle of new
  carrots
25g (1 oz) butter
1 egg yolk
15ml (1 table-
  spoon) cream
Pepper
Salt

*Method*

1. Boil the carrots in salted water for 20–30 minutes until tender.

2. Drain well, take them in a coarse cloth and rub gently to remove the skins.

3. Return to the saucepan with the butter and the pepper and salt. Beat up the egg yolk with the cream, and stir this mixture into the carrots until it thickens.

4. Arrange the carrots in a hot dish, and pour on the sauce to serve.

**T. Foubister, Kirkwall**

# Purée of Turnips

**1.35kg (3 lb)
 turnips**
**60ml (4 table-
 spoons) cream**
**25g (1 oz) butter**
**30ml (2 table-
 spoons) sifted
 flour**
**4 egg whites**
**Parsley**
**Salt**
**Pepper**

## Method

1. Pare and slice the turnips. Put them into a saucepan of cold water, with 2.5ml (half a teaspoon) of salt. Bring to the boil, strain, and rinse in cold water.

2. Now put the slices into fast-boiling salted water and boil until tender.

3. Drain well, dry on kitchen towel, and rub through a sieve.

4. Put this purée into a saucepan with the butter, half the cream, white pepper and salt, and sift in the flour. Stir with a wooden spoon until the mixture boils.

5. Butter a deep fireproof dish and put the purée into it, and pour on 30ml (2 tablespoons) of cream.

6. Add a pinch of salt to the 4 egg whites and whip until stiff. Spread on top of the turnip purée.

7. Stand the dish in a tin of boiling water, and place it in a moderate oven until the egg turns golden.

8. Sprinkle with finely chopped parsley to serve.

**P. Harcus, Kirkwall**

# Baked Mushrooms

**12 mushrooms**
**50g (2 oz) butter**
**Salt**
**Pepper**

## Method

1. Choose large, flat mushrooms. Wipe them with a clean cloth, peel them, and cut off the stalks close up to the crowns. Do not wash them unless absolutely necessary.

2. Butter a fireproof dish and lay the mushrooms edge to edge dark side up. Sprinkle with pepper and salt and put a small piece of butter on each one.

3. Cook in oven for 20 minutes (180°C, 350°F, gas mark 4).

4. Serve piled on a hot dish and pour on the gravy which has run from them.

*T. Gorn, Kirkwall*

## Leeks in White Sauce

4 leeks
White sauce

*Method*

1. Trim off the roots, the outsides, and most of the green.

2. Slit leaves down a little way from the top and wash thoroughly.

3. Place in a saucepan of boiling salted water for 30 minutes until tender.

4. Drain well, halve, and arrange in a hot dish. Serve with white sauce (see p63). Leeks may also be stewed in brown gravy.

*T. Gorn, Kirkwall*

## Aubergine Fritters

1 aubergine
Salt
Frying batter
Frying fat

*Method*

1. Peel a medium-sized aubergine and cut it in slices about 1 cm (1/2 inch) thick. Soak in salt water for 30 minutes then drain thoroughly.

2. Dip the pieces into frying batter, and fry in boiling fat for 5 minutes. Drain on a wire pastry rack.

3. Pile on a hot dish and sprinkle on a little cayenne pepper to serve.

*L. Grieve, Kirkwall*

# Tomato au Gratin

450g (1 lb)
  tomatoes
110g (4 oz)
  breadcrumbs
50g (2 oz) butter
5ml (1 teaspoon)
  chopped
  shallot
5ml (1 teaspoon)
  pepper
5ml (1 teaspoon)
  salt
2.5ml (½ tea-
  spoon) castor
  sugar
110g (4 oz) grat-
  ed cheese

## Method

1. Scald and skin the tomatoes, then cut them in slices.

2. Butter a pie-dish, and line it thickly with buttered breadcrumbs.

3. Put in a layer of tomatoes, sprinkle with pepper, salt, sugar, cheese and a little finely chopped shallot. Cover with a layer of breadcrumbs, tomato, etc, until the dish is full. Finish with a layer of well-buttered breadcrumbs on top.

4. Bake in oven for 30 minutes (190°C, 375°F, gas mark 5).

**L. Allan, Stromness**


# Baked Tomatoes

Tomatoes
  (2 per person)
Butter
Salt
Pepper

## Method

1. Cut out the stalks from the tomatoes.

2. Butter a baking dish, and stand the tomatoes stalk end upwards.

3. Sprinkle seasoning into the hole left by the stalk and add a small piece of butter.

4. Lay a well-buttered paper on top and bake in a moderate oven for 10–15 minutes.

**T. Foubister, Kirkwall**

## Stovies

450g (1 lb) potatoes
Beef dripping or butter
Remains of a brisket of beef
Salt and pepper

### Method

1. Peel and cut the potatoes into 2cm (3/4-inch) slices.

2. Boil a little salted water in a pan and simmer the potatoes until cooked.

3. Dry the potatoes and stir in sufficient beef dripping or butter until they are nicely coated.

4. Shred the ends of the brisket and stir into the potatoes. Season to taste.

5. Serve with oatcakes.

*L. Drever, Stromness*


## Clapshot

Potatoes
Turnip
Carrot
Chives
Butter
Salt
Pepper

### Method

1. Boil equal quantities of potatoes, carrot and turnip. Finely chop the chives.

2. Drain and dry the potatoes, carrot and turnip and mash together with a generous knob of butter. Season well.

3. Sprinkle with the chives to serve.

*L. Drever, Stromness*

# Tatties 'n Cream

900g (2 lb) new
  potatoes
110g (4 oz) but-
  ter
1 onion, chopped
300ml (1 cup)
  single cream
Parsley, chopped
Mint, chopped
Seasoning

## Method

1. Boil the potatoes in their skins,
   drain, peel and dice.

2. Melt the butter in a pan and add the
   onion, parsley, mint and seasoning.
   Stew until the onion is cooked. Mix
   in the potatoes and the cream.

3. Stir until the mixture boils, then
   serve garnished with parsley.

*J. Harcus, Westray*

# Cabbage in Tomato Sauce

1 white cabbage
1 chopped onion
400g (14 oz) tin
  tomatoes
150ml (1/2 cup)
  olive oil
Mixed herbs
Seasoning

## Method

1. Quarter the cabbage and cut out the
   stalk. Blanch in boiling salted water
   for 5 minutes then drain.

2. Cook the onion in the oil then add
   the tomatoes, seasoning and herbs.

3. Put the cabbage into the sauce,
   cover, and simmer until ready.

*W. Harvey, Stromness*

# Creamed Beetroot

20 small beet-
  roots, cooked
  and peeled
300ml (1/2 pint)
  single cream
Chopped chives
50g (2 oz)
  Orkney smoked
  cheese, grated
25g (1 oz)
  Orkney butter

## Method

1. Put the beetroot into a buttered
   oven-dish.

2. Pour on the cream and sprinkle with
   cheese, chives, seasoning and dot
   with knobs of butter.

3. Bake in a hot oven for 15 minutes.

*W. Wylie, Kirkwall*

## Orange Apple Cheese

2 apples
2 oranges
110g (4 oz)
 Orkney cheese

*Method*

1. Peel and core the apples and cut into small pieces.

2. Peel and skin the oranges, divide into segments, and cut each segment into 4 pieces.

3. Roughly grate the cheese and mix with the fruit in a bowl to serve.

**S. Croy, Kirkwall**

## Potato Salad

Potatoes
Onion
Mayonnaise
Parsley

*Method*

1. Chop the potato into small pieces and boil in salted water until just cooked.

2. Dry the potato and stir in sufficient mayonnaise to bind.

3. Finely chop the raw onion and mix into the potato.

4. Garnish with parsley to serve.

**S. Croy, Kirkwall**

## Tomato and Peach

6 tomatoes
220g (8 oz) tin of
 peach slices
Lemon juice
Seasoning
Olive oil

*Method*

1. Peel and slice the tomatoes. Drain the peaches and mix with the tomato.

2. Season with salt and pepper, sprinkle with a little lemon juice and olive oil to serve.

**J. Watt, Kirkwall**

61

## Peach Coleslaw

½ medium cabbage
170g (6 oz) tin of peaches
150ml (½ cup) of sultanas
Mayonnaise

### Method

1. Soak the sultanas in warm water for 30 minutes.

2. Finely chop the cabbage and the peaches. Save the peach juice in a cup.

3. Mix the cabbage, peaches and sultanas together with sufficient mayonnaise to bind.

4. Before serving, pour on the juice of the peaches.

*J. Watt, Kirkwall*

## Egg and Tomato

### Method

An equal amount of hard-boiled egg and tomato mixed to bind with mayonnaise is an ideal addition to a party cold table.

*P. Dennison, Kirkwall*

# SAUCES

## Simple White Sauce

15ml (1 table-
spoon) butter
or margarine
15ml (1 table-
spoon) flour
300ml (½ pint)
hot milk
Salt

### Method

1. Melt the butter in a saucepan over a low heat.

2. Remove from the heat and blend in the flour and salt.

3. Return to heat and cook for 3 minutes without browning, stirring constantly.

4. Remove from the heat and gradually add the hot milk stirring constantly.

5. Return to the heat and cook for another five minutes, stirring constantly until the mixture is smooth and thickened.

6. Blend in a little chopped parsley to serve on fish or vegetables.

## Brown Sauce

15ml (1 table-
spoon) butter
or margarine
15ml (1 table-
spoon) flour
1 stock cube
(beef)
300ml (½ pint)
boiling water
Sprig of parsley
Small bay leaf
Pinch of dried
thyme

### Method

1. Melt the butter in a saucepan over a low heat.

2. Add the flour and cook for 6 minutes until medium brown.

3. Dissolve the Oxo cube in the boiling water and gradually add to the mixture, stirring constantly until thickened and smooth.

4. Add the parsley, bay leaf and thyme and cook over a low heat for 20 minutes stirring occasionally.

5. Strain through a fine-mesh sieve to serve on meat.

63

# Onion Sauce

450ml (1¹/₂ cups)
finely chopped
onions
30ml (2 table-
spoons) butter
or margarine
600ml (2 cups)
hot white sauce
150ml (¹/₂ cup)
double cream

## Method

1. Cover onion with boiling water and stand for 3 minutes.

2. Melt the butter in a saucepan over a low heat.

3. Drain the onion and cook in the melted butter for 5 minutes until soft.

4. Stir into white sauce and simmer for 15 minutes, stirring occasionally.

5. Strain and gradually stir in the cream.

6. Serve with fish, poultry or vegetables.

# Brown Mushroom Sauce

75ml (¹/₄ cup)
sliced mush-
room caps
(reserve stems)
900ml (3 cups)
water
¹/₂ medium onion
¹/₂ stalk celery,
sliced
¹/₂ carrot, sliced
1 parsley sprig
15ml (1 table-
spoon) butter
or margarine
450ml (1¹/₂ cups)
hot brown
sauce
5ml (1 teaspoon)
minced fresh
parsley

## Method

1. Place mushroom stems in saucepan; add water, onion, celery, carrot and sprig of parsley.

2. Simmer over a low heat for 30 minutes.

3. Strain and measure broth. There should be 225ml (three quarters of a cup).

4. Melt butter over low heat.

5. Add sliced mushrooms and cook until tender.

6. Stir in brown sauce.

7. Place over boiling water and heat for 15 minutes.

8. Stir in mushroom stock and minced parsley.

9. Serve with meat and poultry.

# Apple Sauce

450g (1 lb) cooking apples
15g (1/2 oz) butter
30ml (2 tablespoons) water
5ml (1 teaspoon) sugar (if required)

## Method

1. Peel and core the apples and slice them thinly.

2. Put them into a saucepan with the water, cover and cook gently until they turn to a pulp.

3. Beat the pulp with a wooden spoon and add the butter and sugar to taste.

4. Serve on roast pork.


# Bread Sauce

300ml (1/2 pint) milk
50g (2 oz) fine white breadcrumbs
25g (1 oz) butter
1 small onion, chopped
2 cloves
6 peppercorns
Small blade of mace
Cayenne pepper
15ml (1 tablespoon) cream

## Method

1. Put the milk into a saucepan with the onion, cloves, peppercorns, mace and a little cayenne and bring it almost to the boil.

2. Take the pan off the heat and allow the ingredients to fuse for 15 minutes.

3. Strain the milk on to the breadcrumbs and add the butter.

4. Bring the sauce to the boil and add salt to taste.

5. Finally stir in 15ml (a tablespoon) of cream.

# German Sauce

50g (2 oz) flour
50g (2 oz) butter
3 egg yolks
Lemon juice
600ml (1 pint)
  white stock

## Method

1. Melt 40g (1½ oz) butter in a saucepan. Stir in the flour and cook for 3 minutes stirring constantly.

2. Gradually stir in 600ml (1 pint) of well-flavoured white stock until it boils, then let it cook for 10 minutes.

3. Beat the egg yolks in a basin and pour the boiling sauce on to them, stirring all the time.

4. Add a few drops of lemon juice, the remainder of the butter, and serve.


# Reform Sauce

50g (2 oz) flour
25g (1 oz) butter
50g (2 oz) toma-
  toes
1 small onion
600ml (1 pint) of
  brown stock
15ml (1 table-
  spoon) red
  currant jelly
30ml (2 table-
  spoons) Port
  wine
A few drops
  lemon juice
Pepper and salt

## Method

1. Melt the butter in a saucepan. Add the onion, finely chopped, and fry till golden brown.

2. Add the flour and fry until a rich brown.

3. Slice the tomatoes and add them to the above ingredients together with a pint of brown stock. Stir together until it boils and simmer for 45 minutes, then stir in the red currant jelly, wine, lemon juice and the seasoning.

4. Rub the mixture through a fine sieve and reheat to serve.

# Mint Sauce

30ml (2 table-
  spoons)
  chopped mint
Boiling water
10ml (1 dessert-
  spoon) sugar
30ml (2 table-
  spoons) brown
  vinegar

## Method

1. Chop the mint very finely.

2. Melt the sugar with 15ml (one tablespoon) of boiling water in the sauce-boat, add the mint and vinegar.

3. Serve cold on roast lamb.

# Mustard Sauce

1 onion
25g (1 oz) butter
  or margarine
5ml (1 teaspoon)
  dry English
  mustard
300ml (1/2 pint)
  vinegar
15g (1/2 oz) flour
150ml (1/4 pint)
  water

## Method

1. Finely chop the onion and fry in the butter until light brown.

2. Add the flour, then mustard, vinegar and water.

3. Bring to the boil and simmer for 12 minutes stirring frequently.

# Horseradish Sauce

5ml (1 teaspoon)
  mustard
5ml (1 teaspoon)
  vinegar
15ml (3 tea-
  spoons) cream
Salt
Horseradish,
  grated

## Method

Mix the mustard, vinegar and cream together. Add a little salt, and as much grated horseradish as will make a fairly thick consistency.

# Hollandaise Sauce

4 egg yolks
170g (6 oz)
   butter or
   margarine
150ml (1/2 cup)
   boiling water
30ml (2 table-
   spoons) lemon
   juice
2.5ml (1/2 tea-
   spoon) salt
Few grains
   cayenne pepper

## Method

1. Place egg yolks in the top of a double boiler and beat slightly.

2. Heat butter in a saucepan until just melted then gradually blend into the egg yolks.

3. Gradually stir in the boiling water.

4. Cook until thickened, stirring constantly.

5. Remove from the heat and stir in the lemon juice, salt and cayenne.

6. Serve with vegetables, baked or broiled fish, and shellfish.

# Mock Oyster Sauce

3 anchovies,
   chopped
150ml (1/4 pint)
   water
300ml (1 cup)
   cream
Butter
Flour
Mace
Cloves

## Method

1. Simmer the anchovies in the water with a little mace and one or two cloves until anchovies dissolve.

2. Strain the mixture, and when it is quite cool, add the cream. Reheat and thicken with a little butter and flour.

3. To be served on boiled fowl or veal.

# Custard Sauce

300ml (½ pint)
  milk
2 egg yolks,
  beaten
20ml (2 dessert-
  spoons) sugar
Vanilla essence

## Method

1. Heat the milk and pour on to the beaten yolks then strain back into the rinsed pan.

2. Stir over a gentle heat until the mixture thickens but do not boil.

3. Add the sugar and the vanilla essence and mix well.

# Chocolate Sauce

75g (3 oz)
  chocolate
300ml (1 cup)
  icing sugar
300ml (1 cup)
  evaporated
  milk
150ml (½ cup)
  water
5ml (1 teaspoon)
  vanilla essence

## Method

1. Cut the chocolate into small pieces and melt in a double boiler.

2. Stir in the sugar, milk and water. Stir until the sugar has dissolved and the mixture is perfectly blended.

3. Cook slowly for 10 minutes and flavour with vanilla to serve.

# Lemon Sauce

25g (1 oz) butter
30ml (3 dessert-
  spoons) sugar
20ml (2 dessert-
  spoons)
  cornflour
300ml (½ pint)
  water
Grated rind and
  juice of 1
  lemon

## Method

1. Melt the butter in a saucepan.

2. Mix the lemon rind, juice and water into the cornflour.

3. Add the mixture and the sugar to the melted butter and stir well. Bring to the boil and cook for 3 minutes.

69

# Marmalade Sauce

300ml (½ pint) water

Juice and rind of 1 lemon

20ml (2 dessert-spoons) corn-flour

30ml (3 dessert-spoons) marmalade

10ml (1 dessert-spoon) sugar

## Method

1. Put the water and the grated lemon rind into a saucepan and bring slowly to the boil.

2. Mix the lemon juice into the cornflour, add the marmalade and the sugar then the boiling liquid.

3. Return the mixture to the pan for 3 minutes until it thickens.

# Butterscotch Sauce

50g (2 oz) butter

75g (3 oz) granulated sugar

60g (2½ oz) demerara sugar

300ml (1 cup) golden syrup

Pinch of salt

150ml (½ cup) double cream

## Method

1. With the exception of the double cream, mix all the ingredients together in a saucepan.

2. Stir over a low heat until the mixture comes to the boil, then cook slowly for 20 minutes, stirring occasionally. Remove from the heat and allow to cool.

3. Add the cream and beat until smooth.

# DESSERT

## Clootie Dumpling *(to feed six)*

170g (6 oz) self-
  raising flour
75g (3 oz)
  shredded suet
75g (3 oz)
  demerara sugar
1 apple, peeled
  and finely
  chopped
75g (3 oz)
  sultanas
50g (2 oz)
  currants
1 egg
15ml (1 table-
  spoon) mixed
  spice
15ml (1 table-
  spoon) treacle
150ml (1/4 pint)
  sour milk

## Method

1. Mix the ingredients in a bowl in the order given. Warm the milk and dissolve the treacle in it before adding to the mixture to produce a stiff, well-mixed batter. If you stick the mixing spoon in, it should stand upright.

2. Prepare a large pot one third filled with boiling water, put a plate in the bottom, and soak a cotton or linen cloth sufficient in size to hold the batter with the edges gathered up and tied with string.

3. Wring out the boiling cloth, and spread it on your work top.

4. Cover the cloth with a sprinkling of flour and brush evenly over the surface with a pastry brush.

5. Empty the mixture on to the cloth, gather up the edges and tie with a piece of string leaving a little space for the dumpling to swell.

6. Hold the mixture up by the string and smack it all around. This is an important part of the procedure as it adheres the dry flour on the cloth to the batter, which forms a skin round the mixture when it is plunged into the boiling water.

7. Plunge the bag into the boiling water to sit on the plate. The water level should be 5cm (2 inches) below the string.

8. Boil for 2½ hours, keeping a kettle of water on the boil ready to top up to the desired level.

9. Remove the dumpling from the pot, drain, untie, peel back the cloth, and turn upside down on to a serving plate.

10. Place the plate in a low oven for 10 minutes until the dumpling has dried and formed a skin.

11. Serve with milk, cream or custard.

*PS*—Leftovers can be fried in butter the next day and served with a sprinkling of castor sugar.

**Mrs Wallace, Stromness**

## Rhubarb Dumpling

225g (8 oz) flour
110g (4 oz) margarine
2.5ml (½ teaspoon) baking soda
2.5ml (½ teaspoon) cream of tartar
30ml (2 tablespoons) castorsugar
Pinch salt
Milk to mix
Rhubarb
Sugar

*Method*

1. Sieve the flour, sugar, baking soda, cream of tartar and salt.

2. Rub in margarine and make into a paste with milk.

3. Line a greased bowl with the paste.

4. Add some cut rhubarb and sugar.

5. Add another layer of paste, then rhubarb, ending with a layer of paste on top.

6. Cover and steam for 3 hours.

**M. Miller, Stronsay**

## Quick Dumpling

1 jar mincemeat
1 egg
75g (3 oz) self-raising flour

1. Mix mincemeat, flour and egg in a bowl.

2. Put mixture into a well-greased bowl and boil for 2 hours.

**E. Shearer, Finstown**

# Pineapple Pudding

300ml (1 cup) pineapple juice
300ml (1 cup) pineapple cubes
300ml (1 cup) water
Juice of 1 lemon
30ml (2 tablespoons) cornflour
2 eggs, separated
Whipped cream
150ml (½ cup) sugar

## Method

1. Mix the sugar and cornflour together, place them in the top of a double boiler, stir in the pineapple juice, water and lemon juice and cook until smooth.

2. Pour this mixture on to the beaten yolks, fold in the beaten whites, and then add the pineapple cubes.

3. Pour into a buttered baking dish and bake in oven for 20 minutes (160°C, 325°F, gas mark 3).

4. When cool, top with whipped cream to serve.

*L. Flett, Orphir*

# Bread Pudding

225g (½ lb) scraps of bread
15ml (1 tablespoon) sugar
15ml (1 tablespoon) suet
300ml (1 teacup) currants or raisins
5ml (1 teaspoon) ground ginger
300ml (1 teacup) milk
1 egg

## Method

1. Cut crusts from bread and soak in a basin of water for 1 hour.

2. Squeeze out the water and put bread into a dry basin.

3. Add sugar, suet, and fruit.

4. Boil the milk, pour over the dry ingredients and whisk well with a fork.

5. Beat up the eggs and add with the ginger.

6. Butter a pudding bowl, put in the mixture and steam for 1½ hours.

7. Serve with a sweet sauce.

*T. Robertson, Longhope*

# Bread and Butter Pudding

Slices of bread
and butter
50g (2 oz) sugar
3 eggs
900ml (1½ pints)
milk
110g (¼ lb)
sultanas
A grate of
nutmeg

## Method

1. Thickly butter slices of bread and put a layer in the bottom of a pie-dish. Sprinkle on the sultanas and repeat the layers until the dish is full.

2. Boil the milk, and pour it on to the well-beaten eggs. Add the sugar and spice then pour it over the contents of the dish.

3. Bake in oven for 1 hour (160°C, 325°F, gas mark 3).

**P. Firth, Stromness**

# Green Island Seven Cup Pudding

300ml (1 cup)
flour
300ml (1 cup)
breadcrumbs
300ml (1 cup)
suet
300ml (1 cup)
raisins
300ml (1 cup)
currants
300ml (1 cup)
sugar
300ml (1 cup)
milk
5ml (1 teaspoon)
salt
5ml (1 teaspoon)
soda

## Method

1. Mix all dry ingredients together.

2. Add the milk and eggs.

3. Put into a bowl, cover and steam for 3 hours.

**C. Lyon, Stenness**

# Banana Flan

1 flan case
4 bananas
Redcurrant jelly
10ml (1 dessert-
spoon) sugar
150ml (1/2 cup)
whipped cream
Lemon juice
110g (1/4 lb)
black grapes

## Method

1. Mash the bananas, and mix in the sugar, a squeeze of lemon juice and finally the whipped cream.

2. Spread the base of the flan case with redcurrant jelly, spread on the banana mixture and decorate with halved grapes.

**N. Wylie, Kirkwall**

# Graemsay Spiced Apple Tart

**Filling**
3 apples
110g (1/4 lb)
prunes
50g (2 oz) sugar
2.5ml (1/2 tea-
spoon) mixed
spice

**Pastry**
225g (8 oz) flour
110g (4 oz)
margarine
1 egg
15g (1/2 oz) sugar
2.5ml (1/2 tea-
spoon) salt
2.5ml (1/2 tea-
spoon)
cinnamon
Cold water to
mix

## Method

1. Stew the apples, prunes, sugar and spices together.

2. Remove the prune stones and let the mixture cool.

3. Make the pastry by rubbing fat into flour, add dry ingredients, beaten egg and enough water to make a stiff consistency.

4. Set aside a third of the pastry and roll out the rest to line the bottom of your tin.

5. Add the filling, which must be cold.

6. Roll out the remainder of the pastry and put on the top.

7. Bake in oven for 30–40 minutes (180°C, 350°F, gas mark 4).

8. Dust with castor sugar to serve.

**C. Lyon, Stenness**

# Apple Meringue Pie

900ml (3 cups)
hot, sweetened
stewed apples

2.5ml (½ tea-
spoon) grated
lemon rind

2 eggs

30ml (2 table-
spoons) melted
butter

30ml (2 table-
spoons) castor
sugar

110g (4 oz)
shortcrust
pastry

## Method

1. Line a pie-plate with short pastry. Prick the crust over to prevent it from rising, and bake it in the oven 20 minutes (190°C, 375°F, gas mark 5) till crisp and pale golden.

2. Mix the apples with the melted butter, grated lemon rind and the well-beaten egg yolks.

3. Fill this mixture into the pastry shell when it is cold.

4. Beat the whites of the eggs till stiff, beat in two-thirds of the sugar until very stiff, fold in the remainder the sugar, and pile on top of the pie.

5. Put in oven for 10 minutes (160°C, 325°F, gas mark 3) to set.

**L. Allan, Stromness**

# Marmalade Pears

1 large can pear
halves

5ml (1 teaspoon)
butter

170g (6 oz)
sweet orange
marmalade

Whipped cream

## Method

1. Heat the pears in a saucepan. When they are hot, lift them out and keep them warm in the oven.

2. Measure 300ml (half a pint) of the pear juice into a saucepan and cook for 5 minutes. Stir in the marmalade and simmer for a few minutes then remove from the heat and stir in the butter until melted.

3. Pour marmalade mixture over the pear halves and serve at once with whipped cream.

**T. Mackay, Stromness**

# Rhubarb Jelly

450g (1 lb) fresh rhubarb
60g (2½ oz) cornflour
110g (½ lb) castor sugar

## Method

1. Cut the rhubarb into pieces, put in a saucepan, add the sugar and enough water to cover. Stew for 10 minutes until soft.

2. Strain the rhubarb through a cloth. There should be 900ml (1½ pints) of juice. Make up with a little water if short.

3. Mix the cornflour to a smooth cream with a little of the juice. Bring the rest of the juice to the boil and pour it into the mixed cornflour, stirring all the time.

4. Return it to the saucepan, and boil for 3 minutes.

5. Pour into a mould and allow to cool. When cold, turn it out and serve with custard or cream.

**T. Eunson, Kirkwall**

# Apple and Mincemeat Sponge

225g (½ lb) cooking apples
20ml (2 dessertspoons) sweet mincemeat
1 egg
25g (1 oz) margarine
75g (3 oz) sugar
60g (2½ oz) self-raising flour
Milk to mix

## Method

1. Peel and cut apples and place in a pan with 450ml (1½ cups) of water and 25g (1 oz) of sugar.

2. Simmer until tender.

3. Grease a pie dish and put in the stewed apples.

4. Spread the mincemeat over the apples.

5. Beat the margarine and sugar together.

6. Add the egg and flour and beat well. If necessary, add a little milk to make a thick creamy consistency.

7. Pour the mixture over the apples and mincemeat.

8. Bake for 30–40 minutes in oven (190°C, 375°F, gas mark 5).

*J. Wilkie, Evie*

## Banana Charlotte

8 ripe bananas
40ml (4 dessert-
 spoons) apricot
 jam
1 lemon
Slices of bread
50g (2 oz) castor
 sugar
110g (1/4 lb) fresh
 butter
125ml (wine-
 glass) of rum

*Method*

1. Thickly butter a deep pie-dish.

2. Cut a thin piece of bread to cover the bottom of the dish, butter both sides and fit it in.

3. Cut oblong slices of bread, butter on both sides, and line the sides of the mould overlapping slightly.

4. Cut the bananas in half lengthways and then quarter lengthways. Place the pieces in a dish and pour on the 125ml (glass) of rum and the juice of the lemon and let them soak for some time. Sprinkle with sugar.

5. Place a layer of the bananas into the mould and spread a layer of apricot jam on top. Repeat the process until the mould is full.

6. Pour the rum over the bananas in the mould and cover with more slices of buttered bread.

7. Bake in oven for 1 hour (180°C, 350°F, gas mark 4) until brown.

8. Turn out on to a hot dish and serve with custard or cream.

*S. Croy, Kirkwall*

# Trifle

600ml (1 pint)
cream
600ml (1 pint)
custard
6 stale sponge
cakes
12 macaroons
110g (¼ lb)
ratafias
Strawberry jam
300ml (½ pint)
sherry
150ml (¼ pint)
brandy
150ml (¼ pint)
water

## Method

1. Mix the sherry, brandy and water together.

2. Spread a layer of jam on the bottom of the bowl.

3. Cut the cakes in half, dip them into the wine and water, and put a layer on the jam.

4. Dip some macaroons and ratafias in the wine, and put them on the layer of sponge cake.

5. Pour on some of the custard, followed by another layer of jam, soaked cakes and the rest of the custard.

6. Whip the cream and spread on the top.

*P. Firth, Stromness*

# Gooseberry Fool

2.4 litres
(2 quarts)
gooseberries
110g (4 oz) sugar
300ml (½ pint)
cream
300ml (½ pint)
thick custard
Water

## Method

1. Wash the green gooseberries and put them on to boil in half a pint of water. When they turn yellow and are quite soft, turn them out into a coarse sieve over a bowl and press the pulp through the sieve.

2. Stir in 110g (¼ lb) of moist sugar and allow it to cool.

3. When cold, add the custard and cream, and mix thoroughly.

4. Serve in a glass dish, or in melba glasses.

*N. Drever, Kirkwall*

# Pentland Foam

170g (6 oz) sugar
25g (1 oz) butter
2 eggs
40g (1½ oz) flour
1 lemon
180ml (6 oz) milk

## Method

1. Mix sugar, butter, egg yolks and flour together.

2. Add the grated rind of the lemon, the juice of the lemon and the milk.

3. Fold in the egg whites, stiffly beaten.

4. Place in a buttered dish.

5. Set the dish in a tin of hot water.

6. Bake for 40 minutes in oven (160°C, 325°F, gas mark 3).

7. Serve immediately.

**J. Flett, Orphir**


# Surprise Chocolate Cream

½ an orange jelly
½ a packet of marshmallows
1 egg, separated
150ml (¼ pint) milk
30ml (2 tablespoons) drinking chocolate

## Method

1. Dissolve the jelly in 60ml (4 tablespoons) hot water.

2. Stir in the chocolate, and the egg yolk beaten with the milk.

3. Snip the marshmallows into pieces using wet scissors.

4. Fold the stiffly beaten egg whites into the mixture.

5. Put into dish, or dishes, and leave in a cool place to set.

**H. Garson, Sandwick**

# Coffee Sponge

1 tablespoon
  gelatine
1 egg white
30ml (2 table-
  spoons) cold
  water
150ml (1/2 cup)
  castor sugar
900ml (3 cups)
  strong, hot
  coffee
2.5ml
  (1/2 teaspoon)
  vanilla essence

## Method

1. Cover the gelatine with the cold water, and set aside for 10 minutes.

2. Add the sugar and pour on the hot coffee, stirring until the gelatine is dissolved.

3. Let the mixture cool, add the vanilla essence, and when it is about to set, add the egg white beaten to a stiff froth. Beat until spongy and light.

4. Turn into a mould to set, and serve with vanilla or lemon custard.

*N. Eunson, Deerness*

# Strawberry Whip

300ml (1 cup)
  chopped straw-
  berries
10ml (1 dessert-
  spoon) sweet
  sherry
2 egg whites
75ml (1/4 cup)
  castor sugar
150ml (1/4 pint)
  cream
4 whole straw-
  berries
Pinch salt

## Method

1. Chop the strawberries in the morning, add the sherry, then keep in the refrigerator until ready to make the whip.

2. Beat the egg whites with the salt until stiff, then beat in sugar gradually until meringue is stiff and glossy.

3. Whip the cream and fold into the meringue, then lastly fold in the strawberries.

4. Divide into 4 dessert dishes and top with a whole strawberry to serve.

*J. MacLeod, Kirkwall*

## Whisky Pears

450g (1 lb) tin
  pear halves
30ml (2 table-
  spoons)
  Highland Park
Vanilla ice cream
Grated walnut
Chocolate sauce

## Method

1. Strain the juice off the pears and mix in the whisky.

2. Mix the grated walnut into the ice cream.

3. Put two scoops of ice cream on to each plate either side of a pear half and top with chocolate sauce.

4. Pour on the whisky juice before serving.

*J. Dell, Kirkwall*

# BAKING

## *Fruit Cake*

450g (1 lb) self-raising flour
225g (½ lb) margarine
225g (½ lb) castor sugar
450g (1 lb) sultanas
450g (1 lb) raisins
225g (½ lb) glacé cherries
300ml (½ pint) boiling milk
2 eggs, beaten

### *Method*

1. Rub the margarine into the flour.
2. Add sugar and fruit.
3. Pour on the boiling milk and mix well.
4. Add the beaten eggs and mix well.
5. Line an 18cm (7-inch) cake tin and pour in the mixture.
6. Bake for 2 hours in oven (150°C, 300°F, gas mark 2) then reduce the heat to (120°C, 250° F, gas mark 1) for a further 2 hours or until firm.
7. Remove cake from the oven and leave for 10 minutes before turning out onto a cooling rack.
8. This cake is best if kept for 1 month in an airtight tin.

**J. Wilkie, Evie**

## *Fruit Loaf*

110g (4 oz) margarine
110g (4 oz) castor sugar
225g (8 oz) self-raising flour
225g (8 oz) mixed dried fruit
300ml (1 cup) of water
2 eggs
5ml (1 teaspoon) mixed spice
5ml (1 teaspoon) baking soda

### *Method*

1. Put margarine, sugar, fruit, spice and soda into a pan with the water.
2. Simmer this mixture for 5 minutes and leave until cold.
3. Add flour and beaten eggs and mix well.
4. Put into a greased loaf tin and bake for 50 minutes in oven (180°C, 350°F, gas mark 4).

**W. Cursiter, Papa Westray**

## Fruit Slices

450g (1 lb) plain flour
225g (½ lb) margarine
10ml (2 teaspoons) baking powder
1 egg
Pinch of salt
Milk to mix

**Filling**
450g (1 lb) currants
110g (¼ lb) sugar
10ml (1 dessertspoon) mixed spice
Cornflour

### Method

1. Put the currants, sugar and mixed spice into a pan with a little water and cook for 5 minutes.
2. Add as much cornflour as required to make a thick spreading consistency and leave to cool.
3. Rub the margarine into the flour.
4. Add the salt and half of the beaten egg and enough milk to make a stiff dough.
5. Roll out thinly and use half to line the bottom of a Swiss roll tin.
6. Spread the filling on top of this and cover with the rest of the pastry.
7. Brush with the rest of the egg and prick with a fork.
8. Bake for 25 minutes in oven (190°C, 375°F, gas mark 5).

**F. Manson, Dounby**

## Malt Loaf

340g (12 oz) self-raising flour
1ml (¼ teaspoon) cream of tartar
1ml (¼ teaspoon) baking soda
30ml (2 tablespoons) malt extract
25g (1 oz) margarine
2 eggs
30ml (2 tablespoons) syrup

### Method

1. Mix all the dry ingredients together and rub in the margarine.
2. Melt the syrup and malt with 30ml (two tablespoons) of milk.
3. Beat the eggs and pour with the syrup mixture on to the dry ingredients.
4. Stir well, and if necessary, add a little milk to make a soft consistency.
5. Pour into a greased loaf tin and bake for 1–1½ hours in oven (180°C, 350°F, gas mark 4).

**R. Wallace, Shapinsay**

## Grandma's Gingerbread

280g (10 oz)
 plain flour
75g (3 oz) butter
 or margarine
300ml (1 cup)
 of milk
110g (4 oz)
 castor sugar
110g (4 oz)
 treacle
2 eggs
5ml (1 teaspoon)
 mixed spice
5ml (1 teaspoon)
 ginger
5ml (1 teaspoon)
 baking soda
Pinch of salt

### Method

1. Sift the dry ingredients together.

2. Melt the fat with the treacle and add to the mixture with the beaten eggs.

3. Mix to a light batter with the milk and pour into a loaf tin.

4. Bake for 40 minutes in oven (180°C, 350°F, gas mark 4).

*Mrs Groat, Orphir*

## Broonie

170g (6 oz)
 oatmeal
170g (6 oz) flour
110g (4 oz)
 butter or
 margarine
50g (2 oz) sugar
30ml (2 table-
 spoons) syrup
 or treacle
5ml (1 teaspoon)
 ginger
4ml (³/₄ teaspoon)
 baking soda
Pinch salt
1 egg
Buttermilk to mix

### Method

1. Mix meal and flour and rub in fat.

2. Add salt, ginger and soda.  ·

3. Melt the treacle and add together with the beaten egg and sufficient buttermilk to let the mixture drop easily from the spoon.

4. Mix thoroughly and put into a greased tin.

5. Bake for 75 minutes in oven (160°C, 325°F, gas mark 3) or until well risen and firm in the centre.

*B. Leslie, Westray*

## Sanday Bun

110g (4 oz) plain flour
110g (4 oz) self-raising flour
110g (4 oz) margarine
110g (4 oz) sugar
5ml (1 teaspoon) baking soda
5ml (1 teaspoon) cinnamon
450g (1 lb) mixed fruit
2 eggs
25g (1 oz) mixed peel
300ml (1 cup) of water

### Method

1. Put water, sugar, margarine, fruit and soda in a pan and bring slowly to the boil. Boil for 10 minutes.

2. Remove from heat and cool.

3. Add well-beaten eggs, flour and cinnamon and beat well to remove any lumps.

4. Put into a greased loaf tin and bake for 60 minutes in oven (180°C, 350°F, gas mark 4).

**M. Tulloch, Sanday**

## Chocolate Cake with Date Filling

3 eggs
300ml (1 cup) sugar
75ml (5 tablespoons) milk
40g (1½ oz) butter
300ml (1 cup) plain flour
300ml (1 tablespoon) cocoa
5ml (1 teaspoon) baking powder

### Method

1. Beat the eggs and sugar till light and creamy.

2. Put the milk and butter into a pan and bring to the boil.

3. Add the sugar and eggs, flour, baking powder and cocoa.

4. Place in a greased sandwich tin and bake for 20 minutes in oven (180°C, 350°F, gas mark 4).

*Date Filling*

1. Soak 8 dates in hot water with a pinch of soda.

2. Pour off the water and add 25g (1 oz) butter and 15ml (1 tablespoon) of sugar to the dates.

3. Beat until creamy and fill the cake.

4. Ice with chocolate icing.

*J. Muir, Stenness*

## Treacle Scones

225g (8 oz) plain flour
5ml (1 level teaspoon) baking soda
7ml (1 heaped teaspoon) cream of tartar
1ml (1/4 teaspoon) cinnamon
1ml (1/4 teaspoon) ginger
2.5ml (1/2 teaspoon) mixed spice
15ml (1 tablespoon) treacle
Pinch of salt
Milk to mix

### Method

1. Sieve all the dry ingredients together.

2. Add the treacle on a warm spoon with enough milk to form a soft dough.

3. Shape the mixture as required and bake on a hot girdle browning both sides.

*T. Muir, Orphir*

## Rousay Shortbread

340g (3/4 lb) plain flour
110g (1/4 lb) cornflour
225g (1/2 lb) butter
110g (1/4 lb) castor sugar

### Method

1. Mix all the ingredients together and knead into a dough on a cool surface.

2. Roll out to 6mm (1/4 inch) thick, cut into fingers and bake for 40–45 minutes in oven (135°C, 275°F, gas mark 1) until golden brown.

*Oakleigh Hotel, Stromness*

## Ginger Delight

50g (2 oz) butter
150ml (1/2 cup) sugar
1 egg, beaten
150ml (1/2 cup) golden syrup
150ml (1/2 cup) milk
450ml (11/2 cups) flour
5ml (1 teaspoon) ginger
5ml (1 teaspoon) cinnamon
5ml (1 teaspoon) baking soda

*Method*

1. Cream butter and sugar.

2. Add egg, syrup, flour, ginger, cinnamon and soda, and beat well.

3. Add milk and beat again.

4. Divide the mixture into two sandwich tins and bake for 20–25 minutes in oven (180°C, 350°F, gas mark 4).

*H. Garson, Sandwick*

## Fatty Pancakes

225g (8 oz) flour
2.5ml (1/2 teaspoon) baking soda
2.5ml (1/2 teaspoon) cream of tartar
Pinch salt
30ml (2 tablespoons) sugar
2 eggs
170g (6 oz) sultanas or quartered cherries
Milk to mix

*Method*

1. Beat the eggs with the sugar.

2. Mix all the dry ingredients together and add the egg mix with sufficient milk to make a consistency suitable for dropped scones.

3. Mix in the sultanas or cherries.

4. Melt sufficient butter in a frying pan to a depth of 6mm (1/4") and heat till smoking.

5. Drop dessertspoonfuls of batter into the fat and cook quickly on both sides.

6. When both sides are golden brown lift on to a cooling rack and sprinkle with sugar.

*J. MacLeod, Stromness*

## Orkney Oatmeal Scones

300ml (1 cup) plain flour
2.5ml (1/2 teaspoon) baking soda
2.5ml (1/2 teaspoon) cream of tartar
10ml (1 dessertspoon) syrup
10ml (1 dessertspoon) sugar
1 egg
30ml (2 tablespoons) porage oats

### Method

1. Mix all ingredients in a bowl adding water to make a thin consistency.
2. Bake 30ml (2 tablespoonfuls) at a time spread thinly on a hot girdle.

**G. Duncan, South Ronaldsay**

## Clestrain Wheatmeal Scones

225g (8 oz) wheatmeal flour
170g (6 oz) plain flour
5ml (1 teaspoon) baking soda
8ml (1 1/2 teaspoons) cream of tartar
Pinch salt
75g (3 oz) margarine
50g (2 oz) sultanas
15ml (1 tablespoon) treacle
15ml (1 tablespoon) malt extract
1 egg
Milk to mix

### Method

1. Sift all dry ingredients into a bowl of wheatmeal flour.
2. Rub in margarine and add sultanas.
3. Beat malt, treacle, egg and a little milk together and add to dry ingredients.
4. Roll out and cut into shapes.
5. Bake for 15 minutes in oven (220°C, 425°F, gas mark 7).

**J. Muir, Orphir**

# Potato Scones

225g (1/2 lb) cold
  boiled potatoes
15g (1/2 oz)
  butter
50g (2 oz) flour
Salt

## Method

1. Mash the potatoes.

2. Melt the butter and mix with potatoes and salt.

3. Work in as much flour as the paste will take.

4. Roll out very thinly, cut into triangles and place on a hot girdle, pricking well with a fork.

5. Cook for 3 minutes on each side.

6. Can be served hot or cold.

**B. Sutherland, Longhope**

# Crumb Cake

600ml (2 cups)
  S.R. flour
300ml (1 cup)
  castor sugar
170g (6 oz) but-
  ter
5ml (1 teaspoon)
  cinnamon
5ml (1 teaspoon)
  ground cloves
5ml (1 teaspoon)
  baking powder
300ml (1 cup)
  currants
300ml (1 cup)
  sultanas
Buttermilk

## Method

1. Rub the butter into the flour and sugar to a consistency of breadcrumbs.

2. Put aside a quarter of the mixture.

3. Add baking soda, cloves, cinnamon, currants and sultanas to the bulk of the mixture and mix well.

4. Add enough buttermilk to mix to a soft consistency.

5. Put into a lined cake tin and scatter the quarter portion of crumbs on the top.

6. Bake in a moderate oven for 1–1 1/2 hrs.

**Mrs. E.M. Hutchison, Sandwick**

# Raisin Shortbread

60ml (4 table-spoons) orange juice
110g (4 oz) seed-less raisins
170g (6 oz) plain flour
50g (2 oz) castor sugar
110g (4 oz) but-ter

## Method

1. Put the orange juice and the raisins into a small saucepan and bring to the boil. Pour into a bowl and leave to cool.

2. Sieve the flour into a mixing bowl. Add sugar and rub in the butter until the mixture resembles fine breadcrumbs.

3. Knead the mixture thoroughly and divide into two rounds.

4. Place one round on a greased baking tray and spread the raisins over the surface. Top with the second round and press them firmly together.

5. Bake until golden brown (160°C, 325°F, gas mark 3) for 45 mins.

**Mrs. Redland, Sandwick**

# Cream Scones

225g (1/2 lb) flour
5ml (1 teaspoon) baking powder
25g (1 oz) butter
1 egg, beaten
75ml (1/4 cup) sour cream
Pinch of salt

## Method

1. Mix the flour, baking powder and salt in a bowl and rub in the butter.

2. Stir in the egg and sour cream to make a moderately soft dough.

3. Turn out on to a floured board and roll out lightly to 1cm (half an inch) in thickness. Prick all over with a fork, cut into rounds and bake on a girdle or in the oven.

**N. Bruce, Kirkwall**

91

# Girdle Scones

225g (8 oz) flour
2.5ml (1/2 teaspoon) baking soda
5ml (1 teaspoon) cream of tartar
1ml (1/4 teaspoon) salt
25g (1 oz) margarine
Milk to mix

## Method

1. Sieve the flour, baking soda, cream of tartar and salt into a basin.

2. Rub in the margarine and mix in sufficient milk to make a soft dough (not sticky).

3. Turn onto a floured board, divide into four portions and knead each piece lightly.

4. Shape into rounds and roll slightly until the scones are about 6mm (a quarter of an inch) thick, then divide each round into four.

5. Place on a hot greased girdle and bake until golden brown on each side.

6. Serve hot with butter.

*Mrs. E.M. Merriman, Sandwick*

# Smiddy Loaf

110g (4 oz) margarine
110g (4 oz) sugar
225g (8 oz) mixed dried fruit
5ml (1 teaspoon) mixed spice
5ml (1 teaspoon) baking powder
2 beaten eggs
225g (8 oz) S.R. flour
Water to mix

## Method

1. Boil 300ml (a cup) of water in a pan.

2. Add margarine, sugar, mixed dried fruit, mixed spice and baking soda.

3. Simmer for five minutes, then leave till quite cool.

4. Add eggs and flour and mix well.

5. Grease and line a loaf tin and put in the mixture.

6. Bake in a moderate oven for 45 mins.

*Mrs. R. Stanger, Sandwick*

# Orcadian Bere Bannocks

225g (½ lb) flour
225g (½ lb)
  beremeal
5ml (1 teaspoon)
  baking soda
1ml (¼ tea-
  spoon) salt
Buttermilk

## Method

1. Mix all the dry ingredients in a bowl.

2. Add enough buttermilk to make a
   soft consistency.

3. Shape the bannocks on a board with
   beremeal.

4. Bake on a hot girdle till lightly
   browned.

5. Put bannocks on a wire rack and
   cover with cloth while still hot.

**T. Robertson, Longhope**


# Krawen Quarters

450g (1 lb) plain
  flour
5ml (1 teaspoon)
  baking soda
7ml (1 heaped
  teaspoon)
  cream of tartar
75g (3 oz) mar-
  garine
15ml (1 table-
  spoon) syrup
25ml (1½ table-
  spoons) treacle
Pinch of salt
Buttermilk

## Method

1. Sift the dry ingredients into a bowl
   and rub in the margarine.

2. Stir in the syrup and treacle and
   enough buttermilk to make a stiff
   dough.

3. Roll out onto a floured board and
   cut into shapes.

4. Bake for 15–20 minutes in oven
   (245°C, 475°F, gas mark 9).

**B. Drever, Sanday.**

# Papie Oaties

110g (4 oz) plain flour

10ml (2 level teaspoons) baking powder

2.5ml (½ teaspoon) salt

110g (4 oz) rolled oats

50g (2 oz) castor sugar

75g (3 oz) treacle

110g (4 oz) butter or margarine

Coarse oatmeal for decoration

## Method

1. Sift the flour, baking powder and salt together, then add the rolled oats.

2. Put the sugar, treacle and butter into a saucepan and heat until just melted.

3. Cool the mixture slightly, then mix into the flour to form a dough.

4. Sprinkle the surface of the dough with the coarse oatmeal.

5. Press into a greased 18cm (7-inch) sandwich tin and bake for 20–25 minutes in oven (190°C, 375°F, gas mark 5).

6. Cut into wedges before it is cool.

7. Serve with butter and jam or cheese.

*E. Davidson, Papa Westray*

# Grindlay Muffins

900ml (3 cups) flour

300ml (1 cup) sugar

50g (2 oz) butter

5ml (1 teaspoon) baking soda

10ml (2 teaspoons) cream of tartar

Pinch of salt

Milk to mix

## Method

1. Sift flour, baking soda and cream of tartar into a bowl.

2. Rub in butter.

3. Add sugar.

4. Add milk to make a soft consistency.

5. Roll out on a floured board to 6mm (¼ inch) thick.

6. Cut into small rounds and bake on a pre-heated girdle, browning on both sides.

*A. Findlay, Stromness*

# Fatty Cutties

900ml (3 cups)
  plain flour
45ml (3 table-
  spoons) sugar
110g (4 oz)
  currants
225g (8 oz)
  margarine
Pinch of baking
  soda
Pinch of salt

## Method

1. Melt the margarine.

2. Mix the dry ingredients together and add the margarine to form a fairly stiff dough.

3. Roll out on a lightly floured board, shape as required and bake on a hot girdle.

*L. Mathers, Stenness*

# Orkney Pancakes

400ml
  (2 teacups)
  oatmeal
Small quantity of
  sour milk
100ml (1/2
  teacup) flour
10ml (2 tea-
  spoons) syrup
5ml (1 teaspoon)
  baking soda
1 egg
Milk if necessary

## Method

1. Soak oatmeal in a little sour milk for 24 hours.

2. Add the flour, baking soda, syrup and the egg.

3. Beat up, adding milk if necessary, to make a fairly thin consistency.

4. Bake on a hot girdle, browning on both sides.

5. Serve with syrup.

*E. Thomson, Longhope*

## Pancakes

600ml (2 cups) flour
5ml (1 level teaspoon) baking soda
5ml (1 level teaspoon) cream of tartar
15ml (1 tablespoon) sugar
10ml (1 dessertspoon) syrup
1 egg
25g (1 oz) margarine
Milk to mix
2.5ml (1/2 level teaspoon) salt

### Method

1. Melt margarine and syrup.
2. Add to dry ingredients and mix.
3. Add beaten egg and enough milk to make a soft dropping consistency.
4. Bake on a hot girdle browning on both sides.

**M. Groat, Longhope**

## Westray Spice Buns

110g (4 oz) butter
110g (4 oz) sugar
170g (6 oz) plain flour
5ml (1 large teaspoon) ginger
2.5ml (1/2 teaspoon) mixed spice
15ml (1 tablespoon) treacle
15ml (1 tablespoon) sweet milk
2.5ml (1/2 teaspoon) baking powder
2 eggs

### Method

1. Cream the butter and sugar together.
2. Add the dry ingredients, then the milk, treacle and beaten eggs.
3. Mix into a soft consistency and spoon into bun tins.
4. Bake for 20–25 minutes in oven (180°C, 350°F, gas mark 4).

**L. Mathers, Stenness**

## Caramelitas

140g (5 oz)
  margarine
170g (6 oz) plain
  flour
110g (4 oz)
  crushed oats
1ml (1/4 tea-
  spoon) baking
  powder
110g (4 oz
  brown) sugar
1ml (1/4 tea-
  spoon) salt
60ml (4 table-
  spoons) golden
  syrup
170g (6 oz) plain
  chocolate
110g (4 oz)
  chopped wal-
  nuts

## Method

1. Melt 75g (3 oz) of the margarine in a pan and stir in 110g (4 oz) of the flour with the oats, baking powder, sugar and salt.

2. Blend well, and press the mixture into the base of a well greased 23cm (9-inch) square tin.

3. Bake for 10 minutes in oven (180°C, 350°F, gas mark 4).

4. Melt the remaining margarine with the syrup and chocolate.

5. Stir in the remaining flour and add the walnuts.

6. Pour the mixture over the biscuit base and continue to cook for 20–25 minutes.

*M. Butcher, South Ronaldsay*

## Twatt Cinnamon Buns

170g (6 oz) self-
  raising flour
75g (3 oz) mar-
  garine
75g (3 oz) sugar
75g (3 oz)
  chopped dates
10ml (1 dessert-
  spoon)
  marmalade
5ml (1 teaspoon)
  cinnamon
1 beaten egg

## Method

1. Rub the margarine into the flour.

2. Add the sugar, cinnamon, chopped dates, marmalade and the beaten egg.

3. Stir well and form into buns.

4. Bake on a greased tray in oven for 15 minutes (190°C, 375°F, gas mark 5).

*J. Isbister, Twatt*

## Shortbread

110g (4 oz) flour
110g (4 oz) rice flour
110g (4 oz) castor sugar
110g (4 oz) butter
½ a beaten egg
2 tablespoons cream

## Method

1. Sieve the flour and rice flour into a basin, and rub in the butter.

2. Mix in the sugar and bind with the egg and cream.

3. Roll out thinly, cut into fingers and prick with a fork.

3. Bake in oven for 16 minutes (160°C, 325°F, gas mark 3) until brown.

4. Cool on a wire rack.

**N. Kirk, Kirkwall**

## Crunchy Biscuits

340g (12 oz) plain flour
280g (10 oz) margarine
340g (12 oz) soft brown sugar
170g (6 oz) demerara sugar
Pinch of salt

## Method

1. Cream margarine and sugar together.

2. Add the flour and salt to form a dough.

3. Knead lightly, then shape into two rolls approximately 21cm (8 inches) long.

4. Sprinkle sugar on greaseproof paper, roll the dough in the sugar and wrap it in a clean sheet of greaseproof paper.

5. Place in a refrigerator for about 30 minutes.

6. Cut into 6mm (¼ inch) slices and bake for 12–15 minutes in oven (160°C, 325°F, gas mark 3).

**M. Butcher, South Ronaldsay**

# Manse Biscuits

90g (3½ oz) self-raising flour
75g (3 oz) rolled oats
170g (6 oz) demerara sugar
170g (6 oz) margarine
1ml (¼ teaspoon) baking soda
10ml (1 dessertspoon) water

## Method

1. Mix the flour, rolled oats and sugar together.

2. Melt the margarine over a low heat and mix into the dry ingredients.

3. Dissolve the baking soda in water and add to the mixture.

4. Blend well, cover, and leave in a cool place for 4–6 hours.

5. Knead the mixture into a dough, roll out and cut into circles.

6. Bake for 12–15 minutes in oven (150°C, 300°F, gas mark 2) till brown.

**L. Tomison, South Ronaldsay**

# Birsay Biscuits

340g (12 oz) self-raising flour
110g (4 oz) bere (or bran)
225g (8 oz) castor sugar
225g (8 oz) margarine
1 egg
170g (6 oz) sultanas
A good pinch of salt

## Method

1. Cream sugar and margarine.

2. Sieve in flour, add bere, sultanas, egg and salt, and mix well.

3. Turn out on to a floured board, knead into a dough, roll out and cut into large biscuit shapes.

4. Grease a tray and bake the biscuits on the top shelf for 16 minutes (180°C, 350°F, gas mark 4).

5. Transfer from the baking tray to the cooling rack with a fish lifter, as the biscuits will still be soft, but will become crisp as they cool.

**J. Scott, Birsay**

## Caramel Squares

170g (6 oz) flour
110g (4 oz) margarine
5ml (1 teaspoon) syrup
5ml (1 teaspoon) baking powder
75g (3 oz) brown sugar
140g (5 oz) mixed fruit
25g (1 oz) chopped nuts
1 egg
2.5ml (1/2 teaspoon) vanilla essence
Pinch salt

*Icing*
300ml (1 large cup) of sugar
150ml (1/2 cup) creamy milk
15ml (1 tablespoon) butter

*Method*

1. Melt the margarine with the sugar and syrup and beat well.

2. When cool, beat again, and add dry ingredients, vanilla, and finally the beaten egg.

3. Put in a shallow greased baking tin and bake for 30 minutes in oven (180°C, 350°F, gas mark 4).

4. Leave the cake to cool.

5. Prepare the icing by boiling the sugar, milk and butter together, stirring the mixture until it thickens, and spread over the cake while the icing is still warm.

6. Cut into squares.

**L. Mathers, Stenness**

## Crunchy Flapjacks

75g (3 oz) margarine
15ml (1 tablespoon) syrup
15ml (1 level tablespoon) castor sugar
200g (7 oz) Kelloggs Country Store

*Method*

1. Melt butter, syrup and sugar gently in a pan.

2. Remove from heat and mix in country store.

3. Press into a greased 18cm (7") tin and bake for 20–25 minutes in oven (180°C, 350°F, gas mark 4).

4. Leave in tin to cool, then cut into bars.

**M. Leslie, Sanday**

# Unbaked Butterscotch Cookies

225g (8 oz) sugar
170g (6 oz)
  butter or
  margarine
75g (3 oz) can
  evaporated
  milk
140g (5 oz)
  rolled oats
1/2 packet of
  instant butter-
  scotch or
  caramel whip

## Method

1. Put the sugar, butter and evaporated milk into a large pan and bring gently to the boil.

2. Remove from the heat and add the instant whip and rolled oats.

3. Beat thoroughly together.

4. Leave to cool for 15 minutes.

5. Drop teaspoonfuls on to a greaseproof paper lined tray and leave to set.

*H. Garson, Sandwick*


# Rice Biscuits

2 egg yolks
2 egg whites
40g (1 1/2 oz)
  castor sugar
40g (1 1/2 oz)
  flour
5ml (1 teaspoon)
  ground rice
Pinch of cream
  of tartar
Pinch of baking
  soda

## Method

1. Beat the egg yolks and sugar until thick.

2. Add the egg whites and beat again until very thick.

3. Add the dry ingredients and mix well.

4. Drop spoonfuls on to a greased tray.

5. Bake in oven for 12 minutes (160°C, 325°F, gas mark 3).

6. Cool on a wire rack.

*S. Laird, Kirkwall*

# Chocolate Crunchies

110g (4 oz) plain
   chocolate
110g (4 oz)
   crushed sweet
   biscuits
Knob of butter
1 egg, beaten
50g (2 oz) raisins
12 paper cake
   cases

## Method

1. Melt the chocolate in a bowl over hot water.

2. Crush the biscuits.

3. Add the butter to the melted chocolate. Take off the heat and add the biscuit crumbs, egg and raisins. Mix well.

4. Put a dessertspoonful of the mixture into each case and allow to set.

**J. Dell, Kirkwall**

# Cinnamon Biscuits

90g (3½ oz)
   flour
2.5ml (½ tea-
   spoon) ground
   cinnamon
1ml (¼ tea-
   spoon) baking
   powder
50g (2 oz) sugar
50g (2 oz) butter
½ egg
Milk if required
Jam

## Method

1. Mix the dry ingredients together; rub in the butter, add the half egg and mix to a firm paste.

2. Roll out thinly and cut into rounds.

3. Bake for 15 minutes in oven (150°C, 300°F, gas mark 2).

4. Allow to cool, then sandwich two together with jam.

**B. Peace, Kirkwall**

# Lemon Biscuits

225g (8 oz) flour
110g (4 oz) butter
110g (4 oz) sugar
1 egg yolk
Rind of 1 lemon, grated

## Method

1. Cream the butter with the sugar, add the lemon rind and egg yolk and beat well.

2. Mix in the flour to make a soft, light dough.

3. Roll out thinly and cut into rounds.

4. Bake in oven (160°C, 325°F, gas mark 3) until golden brown.

**J. Scott, Birsay**

# Crunchy Peanut Cookies

50g (2 oz) soft butter
50g (2 oz) crunchy peanut butter
80g (3 oz) soft brown sugar
5ml (1 teaspoon) vanilla essence
140g (5 oz) self-raising flour

## Method

1. Heat oven (180°C, 350°F, gas mark 4).

2. Cream the butter, peanut butter, sugar and vanilla essence together until light and fluffy then stir in the flour with a fork.

3. Divide into 30 equal amounts and transfer to a greased baking tray spaced to allow spread.

4. Flatten the portions with a fork then bake in oven for 12 minutes.

**J. Watt, Kirkwall**

# PRESERVES

## Beetroot Chutney

900g (2 lb)
  cooked beetroot
900g (2 lb)
  peeled and
  cored apples
450g (1 lb) onions
225g (½ lb)
  raisins
225g (½ lb)
  sultanas
225g (½ lb) sugar
10ml (2 tea-
  spoons) ground
  ginger
10ml (2 tea-
  spoons) cinna-
  mon
600ml (1 pint)
  vinegar
Salt

*Method*

1. Dice the beetroot into a large basin.

2. Finely chop the apples and onion and cook gently in the vinegar.

3. Add the fruit, spices, sugar and salt and simmer gently for 15 minutes.

4. When the mixture has cooled, mix carefully with the beetroot in the basin.

5. Spoon into prepared jars and cover tightly.

**H. Garson, Sandwick**

## Westfield Chutney

450g (1 lb)
  tomatoes
450g (1 lb) onions
450g (1 lb) apples
450g (1 lb) prunes
900g (2 lb)
  brown sugar
600ml (1 pint)
  vinegar
10ml (2 tea-
  spoons) dry
  mustard
50g (2 oz) salt

*Method*

1. Skin and chop tomatoes, onions, apples and stone and chop the prunes.

2. Put all the ingredients except the vinegar into a pan and heat slowly until the sugar is dissolved then simmer for a further 30 minutes.

3. Add the vinegar and cook for another 30 minutes.

4. Pour into prepared jars, allow to cool, then cover tightly.

**M. Lyon, Stromness**

## Rhubarb and Orange Chutney

600ml (1 pint) vinegar
900g (2 lb) brown sugar
900g (2 lb) rhubarb
450g (1 lb) onions
340g (3/4 lb) sultanas
5ml (1 teaspoon) ground ginger
2.5ml (1/2 level teaspoon) mixed spice
30ml (2 tablespoons) undiluted orange squash
Salt

### Method

1. Cut the rhubarb into small pieces and chop the onion.

2. Put all the ingredients into a pan.

3. Heat gently and simmer for 45–50 minutes or until the mixture thickens.

4. Pour into prepared jars, allow to cool, then cover tightly.

*M. Flett, Birsay*

## Cauliflower Chutney

2 large cauliflower
450g (1 lb) onions
450ml (3/4 pint) vinegar
225g (1/2 lb) sugar
15ml (2 heaped teaspoons) curry powder
5ml (1 teaspoon) all spice
10ml (2 teaspoons) dry mustard
15ml (2 heaped teaspoons) turmeric
Salt

### Method

1. Break the cauliflower into small pieces and chop the onion finely.

2. Put both these ingredients into a bowl, sprinkle with salt and leave to stand overnight.

3. Bring the vinegar to the boil then add the sugar, cauliflower and the spices.

4. Boil for 30 minutes, then, if required, thicken with a little cornflour mixed in cold vinegar.

5. Spoon into prepared jars, allow to cool, then cover tightly.

*B. Coghill, Birsay*

## Gooseberry Chutney

900g (2 lb) green
  gooseberries
110g (¼ lb)
  onions
110g (¼ lb)
  sultanas
450g (1 lb)
  demerara sugar
5ml (1 teaspoon)
  cayenne pepper
10ml (2 tea-
  spoons) ground
  ginger
10ml (2 tea-
  spoons) salt
600ml (1 pint)
  malt vinegar

### Method

1. Top and tail the gooseberries and chop up the onion.

2. Put all the ingredients in a pan and simmer gently for 1½ hours or until the gooseberry skins are tender.

3. Pour into prepared jars, allow to cool, then cover tightly.

4. This chutney improves if kept for a while.

*E. Williams, Orphir*

## Pomona Pickle

450g (1 lb)
  stoned dates,
  finely chopped
450g (1 lb)
  onions, finely
  chopped
450g (1 lb) cook-
  ing apples,
  grated
450g (1 lb)
  demerara sugar
5ml (1 teaspoon) dry
  English mustard
2.5ml (½ teaspoon) salt
2.5ml (½ teaspoon)
  pepper
600ml (1 pint) malt
  vinegar

### Method

1. Mix the dry ingredients together in a bowl.

2. Mix in the malt vinegar.

3. Leave uncovered overnight.

4. Pour into jars and seal tightly.

*L. Whitie, Kirkwall*

# Rhubarb Jam with Cloves

3kg (7 lb) rhubarb
3kg (7 lb) sugar
A few cloves

## Method

1. Cut the rhubarb into 2.5cm (1-inch) pieces, cover with the sugar, and stand overnight.

2. Tie the cloves in a muslin bag and place in a jelly-pan with the rhubarb and sugar and boil for 1½ hours. Remove the bag of cloves and test the jam to set.

3. Pour into prepared jars to cool, then cover tightly.

**Oakleigh Hotel, Stromness**

# Apricot Jam

450g (1 lb) dried apricots
1.8kg (4 lb) sugar
2.1 litres (3½ pints) boiling water

## Method

1. Wash and quarter the apricots.

2. Pour the boiling water over them and stand for 24 hours.

3. Boil in a pan for 1 hour, add the sugar, and boil for another 30 minutes.

4. Pour into prepared jars and cover tightly.

**H. Garson, Sandwick**

# Banana Jam

12 large bananas (not too ripe)
6 sweet oranges
4 lemons
340g (3/4 lb) sugar for every 450g (pound) of bananas

## Method

1. Peel the bananas and cut them into thin slices.

2. Squeeze the juice from the oranges and lemons.

3. Put the bananas, fruit juice and sugar into a large pan.

4. Boil slowly for 45 minutes.

5. Skim, test, and when ready, pour into prepared jars and cover tightly.

**H. Garson, Sandwick**

# Cherry Currant Jam

900g (2 lb) cherries
675g (1 1/2 lb) red currants
1.1kg (2 1/2 lb) sugar
300ml (1 cup) water

## Method

1. Wash the currants and put them in a pan with the water and heat gently, mashing them with a wooden spoon.

2. Simmer for 10 minutes or till all juice is extracted, then strain through a jelly-bag obtaining as much juice as possible.

3. Put the juice in a pan with the stoned cherries and simmer for 10 minutes.

4. Add the sugar and stir till dissolved and boiling.

5. Boil briskly for 10–15 minutes or till jam sets when tested.

**A. Petrie, Stromness**

## Four-Fruit Jelly

Equal quantities of

Cherries
Strawberries
Red currants
Raspberries

450g (1 lb) of sugar to each 450g (lb) of juice

## Method

1. Prepare fruits and put them in a double saucepan and simmer for 1½ hours, crushing and mashing occasionally to extract the juice.

2. When the fruit is quite soft, strain off the juice through a jelly-bag.

3. Measure the quantity of juice and put it in a jelly-pan with the proportionate amount of sugar and stir till dissolved and boiling.

4. Boil briskly for 10–15 minutes till jelly sets when tested.

**L. Laughton, Kirkwall**

## Strawberry and Rhubarb Jam

1.35kg (3 lb) strawberries
900g (2 lb) red rhubarb
1.7kg (3¾ lb) sugar
5ml (1 teaspoon) citric acid

## Method

1. Cut the rhubarb into inch pieces and layer in a basin with the strawberries and sugar overnight.

2. Turn into a jelly-pan, add the citric acid and stir with a wooden spoon over moderate heat until boiling.

3. Boil for 15 minutes then test to set.

**L. Laughton, Kirkwall**

## Blackcurrant Jam

900g (2 lb)
  blackcurrants
1.6kg (3½ lb)
  sugar
1.2 litres (2
  pints) water

## Method

1. Stalk and wash the currants (note that the green bud should not be removed as this improves the flavour and set of the jam).

2. Put the fruit in a pan with the water and boil for 15 minutes keeping up the quantity to at least two-thirds of the original.

3. Add the warmed sugar and stir till boiling. Boil briskly until jam sets when tested (approximately 10 minutes).

**S. Laird, Kirkwall**

## Marmalade

900g (2 lb) mar-
  malade oranges
2 lemons
2.4 litres (4
  pints) water
2.7kg (6 lb)
  sugar

## Method

1. Cut or mince the fruit finely and soak for 24 hours in the water. Keep the pips and centre pith separate in a small bowl covered with water.

2. After soaking the pips, tie them securely in a muslin bag and boil them with the fruit for 1½ hours, or until the peel is tender and the liquid reduced by half.

3. Remove the bag of pips.

4. Add the sugar and bring back to the boil.

5. Test for set after 15 minutes.

6. When ready, pour into prepared jars and cover tightly.

**B. Wick, Sandwick**

# Lemon Marmalade

Lemons
Sugar
Water

## Method

1. Slice the lemons very thinly and remove the pips.

2. To each 450g (pound) of sliced fruit add 1.8 litres (3 pints) of cold water and let it stand for 24 hours.

3. Put the lemon and water into a pan, and boil until the lemon is tender. Pour it all into a large bowl and let it stand until the next day.

4. Measure the lemon and water, and to each 600ml (pint) add 675g (1½ lbs) sugar.

5. Boil together until the syrup jellies. Test on a cold plate.

*I. Flett, Kirkwall*

# Grapefruit Marmalade

4 grapefruits
4 lemons
4 pints water
Sugar

## Method

1. Put the 4 grapefruits into a pan with sufficient cold water to cover them. Bring to the boil and cook slowly until they are tender and can be easily pierced with a fork.

2. Remove the pan from the heat and leave it to stand overnight.

3. Cut the lemons in half, squeeze out the juice and strain it into a basin. Add the pips, tied in a piece of muslin, together with the rind of the lemon thinly sliced. Pour on 2.4 litres (4 pints) of water and leave it to stand overnight.

4. Drain the grapefruit from the water,

cut them in half, scoop out the pulp, put it in a strainer and squeeze out all the juice, discarding the pips and the pulp, but retain the rind, which should be thinly sliced and put in the jelly-pan with the juice of the grapefruits and lemons.

5. Boil slowly until the liquid is reduced by half.

6. Measure the fruit, and for each 600ml (pint) allocate 675g (1½ lb) sugar.

7. Bring the fruit back to the boil, add the sugar, stirring constantly until it has dissolved, then boil slowly until the marmalade will set when tested on a cold saucer.

*L. Craigie, Kirkwall*

## Orange Marmalade

9 Seville oranges
2 sweet oranges
2 lemons
Sugar
Water

*Method*

1. Cut the fruit across into thin slices. Put the pips aside, cover the fruit with 5 litres (9 pints) of cold water and let it stand for 24 hours.

2. Put the fruit into a jelly pan, add the pips tied in a muslin bag, and boil gently for about 1 hour, or until it has been reduced by half.

3. Strain through a jelly-bag or clean cloth and allow to drip overnight.

4. Measure the juice, and to each 600ml (pint) add 450g (1 lb) of sugar.

5. Boil and test on a cold saucer until the marmalade will set.

*L. Craigie, Kirkwall*

# Apple Marmalade

Cooking apples
Sugar
Cloves
Lemon peel
Water

## Method

1. Peel, core and thinly slice the apples.

2. Allow 340g (¾ lb) of loaf sugar for each 450g (lb) of prepared apples.

3. Put the sugar into the preserving pan with a little water (150ml (half a cup) to 2.7kg (6 lb) sugar), let the sugar melt, then boil it for 10 minutes.

4. Put in the prepared apple, with a few cloves and a little lemon peel and boil for 1 hour. Stir and skim well.

5. It should now be completely smooth, fairly clear and a bright amber colour. Test on a cold plate to set.

**P. Miller, Kirkwall**

# Lemon Curd

80g (3 oz) butter
225g (8 oz) sugar
3 eggs
Grated rind of
1 lemon
Juice of two
lemons
10ml (2 tea-
spoons) corn-
flour

## Method

1. Melt the butter gently over a low heat.

2. Add the sugar and rind and heat slowly until the sugar has melted.

3. Add the cornflour with the lemon juice.

4. Remove the pan from the heat, beat the eggs, and stir in slowly.

5. Heat the mixture until it thickens but do not allow to boil.

6. Put into prepared jars, allow to cool, then cover tightly.

**H. Garson, Sandwick**

# CONFECTIONERY

## Tablet

110g (4 oz)
  butter
1.35kg (3 lb)
  sugar
225g (8 oz) tin
  condensed milk
300ml (1 cup)
  milk
300ml (1 cup)
  water
Vanilla essence

### Method

1. Melt the butter in a saucepan, add sugar, water and plain milk and bring slowly to boil for 5 minutes. Remove from the heat and leave for 5 minutes.

2. Add the condensed milk and, stirring occasionally, cook slowly until a little dropped into cold water forms a caramel consistency.

3. Add 5ml (1 teaspoon) of vanilla essence.

4. Remove from heat, beat thoroughly with a wooden spoon, then pour into a greased tin.

5. Mark into squares when nearly cold.

**J. Bain, Westray**

## Treacle Toffee

110g (1/4 lb)
  butter
225g (1/2 lb)
  treacle
225g (1/2 lb)
  demerara sugar

### Method

1. Put the butter into a saucepan, and when partially melted, add the treacle and the sugar. Mix well together, then boil for 8–10 minutes.

2. Test by dropping a little into cold water. If it immediately hardens and is brittle, it is ready to pour out on to a buttered tray.

3. Before it is hard, mark into squares with the back of a knife.

**N. Anderson, Kirkwall**

## Butterscotch

225g (8 oz)
demerara sugar
50g (2 oz) butter
300ml (1 cup)
water
15ml (1 table-
spoon) vinegar

### Method

1. Mix all the ingredients in a pan and heat gently until the sugar dissolves.

2. Boil briskly for 5 minutes without stirring until the mixture thickens and turns golden brown.

3. Test a little of the mixture in cold water, if it sets, pour into a greased tin and cut into squares just before it sets.

**N. Kirk, Kirkwall**


## Barley Sugar

675g (1½ lb)
castor sugar
½ white of
1 egg
300ml (½ pint)
of water
5ml (1 teaspoon)
lemon juice

### Method

1. Put the sugar into a saucepan with the water and egg white and mix well.

2. Bring to the boil and skim carefully. As soon as the scum ceases to rise, the sugar is clarified.

3. Boil until a little dropped into cold water becomes hard and brittle.

4. Remove from the heat, mix in the lemon juice, let it stand for a minute, then pour on to an oiled tray. Before it sets hard, cut into strips and twist them.

**N. Anderson, Kirkwall**

# Royal Fudge

450g (1 lb)
  brown sugar
300ml (1 cup)
  walnuts
Knob of butter
Grated rind of 1
  orange

## Method

1. Put all the ingredients into a saucepan, stir until the sugar has dissolved and the mixture comes to the boil.

2. Boil for 3 minutes. Remove the pan from the heat and beat the mixture until it thickens.

3. Pour into a buttered tin and cut into squares when cold.

**L. Allan, Stromness**

# Peppermint Creams

675g (1½ lb)
  icing sugar
1 egg white
Water
Peppermint
  essence

## Method

1. Put the egg white and an equal quantity of water in a bowl with a little peppermint essence and gradually add sufficient icing sugar to make a stiff dough.

2. Roll out the dough to 6mm (a quarter of an inch) in thickness and cut into small rounds. Place on a smooth tray dusted with icing sugar to dry. Ready to eat in 12 hours.

**T. Findlay, Stromness**

116

## Fruit Cream Bars

675g (1½ lb)
  icing sugar
1 egg white
Water
Preserved fruits
Assorted fruits

### Method

1. Put the egg white and an equal quantity of water in a bowl and gradually add sufficient icing sugar to make a stiff dough.

2. Chop up some assorted preserved fruits such as glacé cherries, figs, raisins and a little peel. Work this into the sugar cream, then roll out to 2cm (three quarters of an inch) thick.

3. Cut into bars and place to dry on a smooth tray dusted with icing sugar. Ready to eat in 12 hours.

***T. Findlay, Stromness***


## Candied Orange

1 tin of man-
  darin oranges
225g (½ lb) cane
  sugar
150ml (¼ pint)
  water

### Method

1. Strain the juice off the oranges and dry them on kitchen paper.

2. Boil the sugar and the water to the 'crack'. This is when a little dropped into cold water sets hard and brittle. Remove from the heat.

3. Stick each piece of orange on a skewer and dip it into the syrup. Remove any strands hanging beneath, and lay the oranges on a tray to set.

***L. Wallace, Kirkwall***

# HOME BREW

## Home-brewed Ale

The secrets of real Orkney home brewed ale are, I suspect, as lost nowadays as the famous heather ale of the R. L. Stevenson ballad. I have tasted it once or twice in the 1940s—a marvellous unforgettable experience.

In the late twentieth century, nearly everything is second-rate; easily achieved, soon to be discarded. The beauty of craftsmanship—'a joy for ever'—is unknown in these giddy shallow whirling times.

This is not to say that 'instant home-brew' is not worth drinking. I know brewers who make excellent ale out of extract of malt and sugar. But it resembles real ale as a cleverly-taken photo resembles an old master.

## What to do

Buy a plastic dustbin, capacity 20 litres (4 gallons) or thereby.

Decant into it a 900g (2 lb) or 1.1kg (2½ lb) tin of hop-flavoured extract of malt. It lies there like dark sweet lava. Over the lava pour a 900g (2 lb) poke of sugar; frosted snow, it lies on the lava: impotent as yet.

With a kettle of warm water dissolve the malt extract and the sugar, stirring at first stickily and at last fluently with a wooden spoon.

Add 10ml (a couple of teaspoons) of salt.

With warm water make up the level to within 7.5 to 10cm (3 or 4 inches) of the top of the bin.

When the sticky rather ugly-looking mixture stands at bloodheat—the same as you and me—sprinkle on the magic ingredient, yeast (you can buy it by the packet, quite cheap).

For a while nothing happens. The grains of yeast swell, coagulate, form a mild mass on the surface of the dark tarn. But a mystery is happening. Lift the lid after a few hours, and a noble saffron head of froth presents itself. Tilt your ear, you can detect a seething, an endless susurration, the song of Barleycorn. The yeast is slowly transforming the malt sugars and cane sugars into alcohol. It is a work not to be hurried; it takes days for

118

the process to work itself out. In summer the merry battle is over faster than in the cold months.

When the yeast has stopped working, and the surface of the liquor looks (again) like a dark inert tarn, the time has come to empty the brew into clean bottles.

Store the full bottles like precious ingots in the vault of the cupboard. Be patient for at least a fortnight. If you have the strength to feast nothing more than your eyes on it for a month or 5 weeks, all the better.

Then, some cold disagreeable evening, blow up the fire, open a couple of bottles, sip, swallow, and behold the squandering in defeat of many of the miseries of this world.

*George Mackay Brown, Stromness*

## Orkney Ale

6.3kg (14 lb) malt
50g (2 oz) hops
675g (1½ lb) sugar
38 litres (8 gallon) water
25g (1 oz) baker's yeast

### Method

1. See that the vessel is spotlessly clean then put in the malt.
2. Bring the water almost to boiling point and pour it over the malt. Cover lightly, and let it mask for 3 hours.
3. Strain the mixture, and add the hops (tied in a muslin bag to save straining) and 450g (1 lb) of sugar. Boil for 1 hour.
4. Return the liquor to the vessel, and when it has cooled to blood heat, add the yeast which may be 'started' by sprinkling with a little sugar or by frothing in a little of the warm liquor then diluted before adding to the vessel to start fermentation.
5. When fermentation has ceased (usually after 2 or 3 days), skim the surface, allow to settle, bottle and cork tightly. 2.5ml (half a teaspoon) of sugar may be added to each bottle if desired.

*F. Marian McNeill*

## Birsay Brew

Heather blossom
Ginger
Hops
Honey or syrup
Yeast
Water

### Method

1. Gather a large quantity of fully bloomed heather blossom.
2. Cover with water in a large pot and boil for one hour.
3. Strain and measure the liquid. For every 7 litres (1½ gallons) of liquid add 25g (1 oz) ginger, 15g (½ oz) hops and 450g (1 lb) of honey or syrup.
4. Boil for 20 minutes.
5. Cool to lukewarm, then add 15g (½ oz) of brewers yeast for every 7 litres (1½ gallons) of liquid.
6. Cover with a cloth until the next day, then skim, bottle and cork loosely for a few days until fermentation has ceased, then cork tightly.
7. Ready to drink after 2 months, but improves with age.

*E. Moar, Dounby*

## Sweet Sherry Wine

1.8kg (4 lb) brown sugar
900g (2 lb) green grapes
450g (1 lb) raisins
6 potatoes thinly sliced
25g (1 oz) fresh yeast
4.8 litres (1 gallon) boiling water

### Method

1. Crush the grapes and add to the boiling water with the potatoes, raisins and sugar.
2. Allow to cool till lukewarm then add the yeast.
3. Cover and stir daily for 3 weeks.
4. Filter and bottle and allow to stand for 3 weeks loosely corked then cork tightly.
5. Ready to drink in 6 weeks.

*H. Garson, Sandwick*

## Tattie Wine

10 medium sized potatoes
1 orange
2 lemons
2.7kg (6 lb) sugar
900g (2 lb) raisins
25g (1 oz) fresh yeast
6 litres (10 pints) boiling water

### Method

1. Wash the potatoes, (do not peel) and cut them into small slices.
2. Cut the unpeeled lemons and orange into thin slices.
3. Put these ingredients into a large vessel, add the raisins and sugar and pour on the boiling water.
4. Allow to stand until lukewarm, then add the yeast.
5. Cover and stir daily for 10 days till quite flat.
6. Strain and bottle. Cork loosely for the first 3 weeks then cork tightly.
7. Ready to drink after 6 months.

**E. Laird, Harray**

## Rhubarb Wine

2.2kg (5 lbs) rhubarb
1.3kg (3 lbs) sugar
2 lemons
25g (1 oz) fresh yeast
4.8 litres (1 gallon) of boiling water

### Method

1. Chop up rhubarb and lemons and add with the sugar to the boiling water.
2. Allow to cool until lukewarm.
3. Spread the yeast on a piece of toast and let it float in the liquid.
4. Cover with a cloth and let it stand for 3 weeks.
5. Strain off the liquid, bottle and cork.
6. Ready to drink after 6 months.

**I. Sinclair, Sandwick**

# Rural Liqueur

750ml (1 bottle)
cider
750ml (1 bottle)
rose-hip syrup
300ml (1 cup)
whisky
170g (6 oz) sugar

## Method

Mix all ingredients together and stir well until the sugar has dissolved. Bottle and keep for 3 weeks before drinking.

**R. Wallace, Shapinsay**

# Athole Brose

450ml (1¹/₂ cups)
double cream
300ml (1 cup)
lightly toasted
oatmeal
150ml (¹/₂ cup)
heather honey
250ml (2 wine
glasses)
Highland Park

## Method

1. Beat the cream to a froth.

2. Stir in the oatmeal, followed by the honey.

3. Just before the serving, mix in the whisky.

**F. Marian McNeill**

# Oatmeal Nog

15ml (1 table-
spoon) oatmeal
15ml (1 table-
spoon)
Highland Park
15ml (1 table-
spoon) honey
300ml (¹/₂ pint)
milk
Pinch of salt

## Method

1. Heat the milk and pour it over the oatmeal in a small bowl. Cover, and leave for 1 hour, then strain, squeezing the meal dry.

2. Return the mealy milk to the pan, add the salt and the honey, bring to the boil and simmer for 10 minutes.

3. Pour into a tumbler, add the whisky, and drink hot.

**F. Marian McNeill**

## Advocat

3 large eggs
3 lemons
450g (1 lb) cas-
   tor sugar
1 large tin evap-
   orated milk
150ml (1/4 pint)
   of brandy

### Method

1. Break the eggs and shells into a basin and cover with the juice of the lemons.

2. Keep turning the eggs in the juice for three days.

3. Strain the eggs and juice through muslin into a large baking bowl.

4. Add the sugar, milk and brandy and whisk together until frothy.

5. Bottle and drink as soon as you like.

**I. Sinclair, Sandwick**

## Cameron's Kick

1/3 Highland Park
1/3 Irish whisky
1/6 lemon juice
1/6 orgeat syrup

### Method

Shake well and strain into cocktail glasses.

**F. Marian McNeill**

## Dewar's Drink

3/5 Highland Park
2/5 ginger wine

### Method

Named after the late Dr James Dewar of St Margaret's Hope, South Ronaldsay, who, after exposure to high gales and wild seas when visiting patients in his island group, would concoct this drink as a restorative.

**F. Marian McNeill**

# HOUSEHOLD HINTS

APPLES—To peel: Drop a few drops of lemon juice into a pan of cold water. As you pare the apples drop them into the water and they will retain their colour.

BACON—To cook: Hold each slice of bacon under the cold water tap for a few seconds, wipe off the water, then lay the bacon in an earthenware or enamel dish, instead of a frying pan, and cook in a hot oven for a few minutes. This method preserves the fat, and the flavour is improved.

CUSTARD—To stop a skin forming on custard, sprinkle the top with sugar.

DRIED BEANS AND PEAS—To boil: Soak overnight in water with a teaspoonful of sodium bicarbonate added. They will retain their colour and be nice and soft.

BREAD—To keep fresh: Wash and dry a large potato and put it in the bottom of your bread bin.

NEW BREAD—To cut: Dip the bread knife in boiling water and new bread will cut quite easily.

BUTTER—To cream: Butter will cream more easily if placed in a basin which has just been rinsed with boiling water.

CABBAGE—To make digestible: When half-boiled, pour off the water and add fresh boiling water.

CAKE—To keep moist: Keep part of a loaf of bread with your cake in a tin with a close fitting lid, and the cake will not get dry.

CAKE—To remove from tin: Place the baking tin in a basin of hot water for a few seconds. The heat loosens the cake and it can then be easily turned out.

CAKE-MAKING HINT—To prevent the fruit from sinking, dredge a little flour over the raisins, etc, before adding them to the rest of the ingredients.

CHEESE—To prevent it turning dry: Wrap it in a damp muslin cloth and sprinkle with vinegar. Keep in a cool, raised covered dish.

DRIPPING—To clarify: Chop the dripping, and put it into a saucepan with enough water to cover well. Let it boil without a lid until the liquid no longer looks milky, but is oily. Let it cool a little, then strain through a coarse piece of calico into a clean basin.

FISH-BONE—To remove: The juice slowly sucked from half a lemon will often remove a fish bone that has become lodged in the throat.

FISHY SMELL—To remove from saucepan: Empty tea leaves into the pan, cover with water; leave for a few minutes, rinse out and all taste or smell of fish will have gone.

GAME—To test if hung: Pull a feather from the lower part of the back near the tail. If it comes out quite easily, the bird is 'high' enough for the average consumer.

GREENS—To boil: Add a piece of fat about the size of your thumb to the water, and it will not boil over.

HAM—An excellent way to boil: Wrap your ham in greaseproof paper and put a small Spanish onion in the water with the ham. When the ham is tender leave it in the water until it is nearly cold to keep the flesh moist and improve the flavour.

JELLY—To set quickly: Stand the mould in a basin. Fill the basin with water reaching nearly to the top of the mould, then put a handful of kitchen salt in the water. The jelly will set in half the usual time.

LETTUCE—To crisp: A few drops of lemon juice added to the rinsing water will make the lettuce crisp.

MILK—To prevent boiling over: Place a wooden spoon in the saucepan of milk just before it comes to the boil and the milk will not boil over.

OMELETTE—Always let the butter be smoking hot before adding your mixture to the pan. This avoids sticking.

PARSLEY—To dry for storage: Take a bunch of parsley, and holding it by the stems, dip it in boiling water until it is a vivid green. Put it in a quick oven to dry. Rub between your hands or through a coarse sieve.

PEELING ONIONS—Begin at the root end and peel upwards, then the odour will scarcely effect your eyes at all.

PEPPER POTS—To prevent clogs: Place a dried pea in the pot and it will prevent the holes in the lid from becoming clogged.

POTATOES—To bake: Potatoes will bake more quickly if they are first allowed to stand in hot water for 15 minutes.

POTATOES, MASHED—A sprinkle of baking powder added to potatoes while mashing makes them much lighter.

POULTRY—To keep fresh: Place a large peeled onion inside the birds that are not to be used or cooked for a day or two.

RICE—To boil: Add a little lemon juice to the water. This makes the rice white and grainy when cooked.

SALT CELLAR—To prevent clogging: Place a few grains of rice in the salt cellar. This will absorb any dampness and prevent clogging.

# INDEX

## A

| | |
|---|---|
| Advocat | 123 |
| Apple and mincemeat sponge | 77 |
| Apple marmalade | 113 |
| Apple meringue pie | 76 |
| Apple sauce | 65 |
| Apricot jam | 107 |
| Athole brose | 122 |
| Aubergine fritters | 57 |

## B

| | |
|---|---|
| Baked beef and bacon loaf | 29 |
| Baked fillets with tomato sauce | 21 |
| Baked mushrooms | 56 |
| Baked Orkney ham with bananas | 34 |
| Baked stuffed Birsay cod | 20 |
| Baked sweetbreads | 35 |
| Baked tomatoes | 58 |
| Balfour beef | 30 |
| Banana charlotte | 78 |
| Banana flan | 75 |
| Banana jam | 108 |
| Barley sugar | 115 |
| Beef brose | 17 |
| Beef olives | 29 |
| Beefsteak and kidney pudding | 27 |

| | |
|---|---|
| Beetroot chutney | 104 |
| Beetroot soup | 14 |
| Birsay biscuits | 99 |
| Birsay brew | 120 |
| Birsay haddock soufflé | 19 |
| Blackcurrant jam | 110 |
| Bread and butter pudding | 74 |
| Bread pudding | 73 |
| Bread sauce | 65 |
| Broonie | 85 |
| Brown mushroom sauce | 64 |
| Brown sauce | 63 |
| Brussels sprouts soup | 14 |
| Butterscotch | 115 |
| Butterscotch sauce | 70 |

## C

| | |
|---|---|
| Cabbage in tomato sauce | 60 |
| Cabbage soup | 9 |
| Cameron's kick | 123 |
| Candied orange | 117 |
| Caramel squares | 100 |
| Caramelitas | 97 |
| Carrots in lemon butter | 55 |
| Carrot soup | 11 |
| Casserole of smoked fish | 21 |
| Cauliflower chutney | 105 |
| Cauliflower soup | 10 |
| Cheese, onion and potato pie | 48 |

| | |
|---|---|
| Cheesy macaroni | 51 |
| Cherry currant jam | 108 |
| Chicken baked in rice | 39 |
| Chicken broth | 11 |
| Chicken stuffed with mushrooms | 37 |
| Chocolate cake with date filling | 86 |
| Chocolate crunchies | 102 |
| Chocolate sauce | 69 |
| Cinnamon biscuits | 102 |
| Clapshot | 59 |
| Clestrain wheatmeal scones | 89 |
| Clootie dumpling | 71 |
| Coffee sponge | 81 |
| Country-style chicken | 37 |
| Creamed beetroot | 60 |
| Cream scones | 91 |
| Crofter's hotpot | 24 |
| Crumb cake | 90 |
| Crunchy biscuits | 98 |
| Crunchy flapjacks | 100 |
| Crunchy peanut cookies | 103 |
| Custard sauce | 69 |

**D**

| | |
|---|---|
| Devilled lobsters | 23 |
| Dewar's drink | 123 |
| Duck with red cabbage | 40 |

**E**

| | |
|---|---|
| Egg and tomato | 62 |

**F**

| | |
|---|---|
| Fatty cutties | 95 |
| Fatty pancakes | 88 |
| Fish casserole | 22 |
| Fish soup | 15 |
| Four-fruit jelly | 109 |
| Fricassée of fish | 26 |
| Fruit cake | 83 |
| Fruit cream bars | 117 |
| Fruit loaf | 83 |
| Fruit slices | 84 |

**G**

| | |
|---|---|
| Gairsay mutton | 32 |
| Game pie | 42 |
| German sauce | 66 |
| Ginger delight | 88 |
| Girdle scones | 92 |
| Gooseberry chutney | 106 |
| Gooseberry fool | 79 |

| | |
|---|---|
| Graemsay partan | 25 |
| Graemsay spiced apple tart | 75 |
| Grandma's gingerbread | 85 |
| Grapefruit marmalade | 111 |
| Green Island seven cup pudding | 74 |
| Grindlay muffins | 94 |

**H**

| | |
|---|---|
| Haddock kedgeree | 52 |
| Hamnavoe pie | 49 |
| Ham toast | 47 |
| Hollandaise sauce | 68 |
| Holm vegetable soup | 8 |
| Home-brewed ale | 118 |
| Home-brew Orkney stew | 27 |
| Horseradish sauce | 67 |

**K**

| | |
|---|---|
| Kippered eggs | 52 |
| Krawen quarters | 93 |

**L**

| | |
|---|---|
| Leeks in white sauce | 57 |
| Lemon biscuits | 103 |
| Lemon curd | 113 |
| Lemon marmalade | 111 |
| Lemon sauce | 69 |
| Lentil soup | 17 |
| Lobster shell soup | 16 |
| Lyonnaise eggs | 45 |

**M**

| | |
|---|---|
| Maeshowe bacon savoury | 47 |
| Malt loaf | 84 |
| Manse biscuits | 99 |
| Marmalade | 110 |
| Marmalade pears | 76 |
| Marmalade sauce | 70 |
| Mint sauce | 67 |
| Mock oyster sauce | 68 |
| Mustard sauce | 67 |
| Mutton cutlets with tomatoes | 31 |
| Mutton fritters | 32 |
| Mutton soup with dumplings | 18 |

**N**

| | |
|---|---|
| New carrots and cream | 55 |
| North Isles savoury | 45 |

**O**

| | |
|---|---|
| Oatmeal nog | 122 |
| Onion sauce | 64 |
| Orange apple cheese | 61 |

Orange marmalade 112
Orcadian oatmeal soup 7
Orcadian bere bannocks 93
Orkney ale 119
Orkney bacon savoury 50
Orkney cheese 54
Orkney oatmeal scones 89
Orkney pancakes 95
Orkney seaside curry 23
Orkney trout crunch 24
Oxtail soup 16
Oyster chicken 38

P

Pancakes 96
Papie oaties 94
Peach coleslaw 62
Peedie pies 34
Pentland Firth pie 20
Pentland foam 80
Peppermint creams 116
Pigeons with rice and
        Parmesan cheese 41
Pineapple pudding 73
Pomona pickle 106
Potato and cheese mould 48
Potato salad 61
Potato scones 90
Potato soup 12
Purée of turnips 56

Q

Quick dumpling 72

R

Rabbit hotpot 40
Rabbit with mustard sauce 44
Raisin shortbread 91
Red potage 8
Reform sauce 66
Rhubarb and orange chutney 105
Rhubarb dumpling 72
Rhubarb jam with cloves 107
Rhubarb jelly 77
Rhubarb wine 121
Rice biscuits 101
Rice with cheese sauce 51
Rousay shortbread 87
Royal fudge 116
Rural liqueur 122

S

Salmon pie 25

Sanday bun 86
Scotch broth 7
Scotch nips 50
Scots kale 13
Scottish herring soup 13
Shortbread 98
Simple white sauce 63
Smiddy loaf 92
Smoked fish supreme 19
Smothered turkey 39
Soused herring 22
Spring soup 9
Stenness ham and tomato pie 35
Stewed breast of lamb 33
Stewed steak and oysters 28
Stovies 59
Strawberry and rhubarb jam 109
Strawberry whip 81
Stronsay veal 36
Stuffed bacon on toast 49
Stuffed cabbage 53
Surprise chocolate cream 80
Sweet sherry wine 120

T

Tablet 114
Tatties 'n cream 60
Tattie wine 121
Toasted giants 46
Tomato and peach 61
Tomato au gratin 58
Tomato soup 10
Treacle scones 87
Treacle toffee 114
Trifle 79
Trout toast 53
Turkey and asparagus 44
Turkey cutlets 43
Twatt cinnamon buns 97

U

Unbaked butterscotch
        cookies 101

W

Wardhill pie 42
Ward speciality 30
Westfield chutney 104
Westray spice buns 96
Whisky pears 82
Winter supper 46
Winter vegetable soup 12

128